Dr. Ackerman's Book of Dachshunds

LOWELL ACKERMAN DVM

BB-115

Overleaf: A miniature smooth, Kelsea, noses her standard longhaired companion, Chanios. Both are owned by Lucy Granowicz.

The author has exerted every effort to ensure that medical information mentioned in this book is in accord with current recommendations and practice at the time of publication. However, in view of the ongoing advances in veterinary medicine, the reader is urged to consult with his veterinarian regarding individual health issues.

Photography by Lowell Ackerman, DVM, Isabelle Francais, Karen Henry, Micheal Kirkpatrick, Judy Nunes, Robert Percy, Vince Serbin, Nancy Sternberg.

The presentation of pet products in this book is strictly for instructive purposes only; it does not constitute an endorsement by the author, publisher, owners of dogs portrayed, or any other contributors.

Distributed in the UNITED STATES to the Pet Trade by T.F.H. Publications, Inc., One T.F.H. Plaza, Neptune City, NJ 07753; distributed in the UNITED STATES to the Bookstore and Library Trade by National Book Network, Inc. 4720 Boston Way, Lanham MD 20706; in CANADA to the Pet Trade by H & L Pet Supplies Inc., 27 Kingston Crescent, Kitchener, Ontario N2B 2T6; Rolf C. Hagen Inc., 3225 Sartelon St. Laurent-Montreal Quebec H4R 1E8; in CANADA to the Book Trade by Vanwell Publishing Ltd., 1 Northrup Crescent, St. Catharines, Ontario L2M 6P5 ; in ENGLAND by T.F.H. Publications, PO Box 15, Waterlooville PO7 6BQ; in AUSTRALIA AND THE SOUTH PACIFIC by T.F.H. (Australia), Pty. Ltd., Box 149, Brookvale 2100 N.S.W., Australia; in NEW ZEALAND by Brooklands Aquarium Ltd. 5 McGiven Drive, New Plymouth, RD1 New Zealand; in Japan by T.F.H. Publications, Japan—Jiro Tsuda, 10-12-3 Ohjidai, Sakura, Chiba 285, Japan; in SOUTH AFRICA by Lopis (Pty) Ltd., P.O. Box 39127, Booysens, 2016, Johannesburg, South Africa. Published by T.F.H. Publications, Inc.
MANUFACTURED IN THE
UNITED STATES OF AMERICA
BY T.F.H. PUBLICATIONS, INC.

CONTENTS

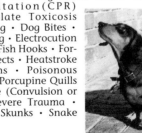

DEDICATION

To my wonderful wife Susan and my three adorable children, Nadia, Rebecca, and David.

PREFACE

Keeping your Dachshund healthy is the most important job that you, as owner, can do. Whereas there are many books available that deal with breed qualities, conformation, and show characteristics, this may be the only book available dedicated entirely to the preventative health care of the Dachshund. This information has been compiled from a variety of sources and assembled here to provide you with the most up-to-date advice available.

This book will take you through the important stages of selecting your pet, screening it for inherited medical and behavioral problems, meeting its nutritional needs, and seeing that it receives optimal medical care.

So, enjoy the book and use the information to keep your Dachshund the healthiest it can be for a long, full and rich life.

Lowell Ackerman DVM

BIOGRAPHY

D r. Lowell Ackerman is a world-renowned veterinary clinician, author, lecturer and radio personality. He is a Diplomate of the American College of Veterinary Dermatology and is a consultant in the fields of dermatology, nutrition and genetics. Dr. Ackerman is the author of 34 books and over 150 book chapters and articles. He also hosts a national radio show on pet health care and moderates a site on the World Wide Web dedicated to pet health care issues (http://www.familyinternet.com/pet/pet-vet.htm).

BREED HISTORY

THE GENESIS OF THE MODERN DACHSHUND

The Dachshund is of German origin, its name meaning "badger dog." Dachshund is the preferred name in the United States but the breed is also known by many other  names in Europe, including Teckels, Tekkels, Dachels, or Dachsels. Although some have claimed that the Dachshund originated in Egypt over 3000 years ago, most acknowledge that the breed likely has a more contemporary history.

Facing page: The Dachshund has been called different names in different countries, but has always been a prized hunter and companion.

The first mention of dogs specifically bred for hunting badgers was made in the mid-16th century. Originally bred as a hunting dog, today's Dachshund is more likely to be a "digger" than a "killer." These affectionate dogs are long on body and short on legs and maintain a devoted following. Originally they were effective at burrowing for badgers, but they were also used against wild boars, foxes, and deer. The German hunters and foresters of the 18th and 19th centuries created the breed to be fearless, tenacious, short and elongated enough to fit into a burrow and do battle with a vicious badger. The standard-sized Dachshunds were bred to engage badgers and foxes; the miniature Dachshunds (Zwergteckel and Kaninchenteckel) were bred for rabbits.

Dachshunds of all sizes were bred to be tenacious and fearless. You can see the concentration on this smooth Dachsie's face.

Mini Dachshunds were bred to go after smaller game, like rabbit. This is a miniature longhaired Dachshund, Ch. Westerly Long Tale of Sharay, owned by Glen Wexler.

The Dachshund has been domesticated for hundreds of years but has only become popular in the United States over the last century or so. The first Dachshunds were brought into the United States in the 1880s and were quite popular for the next 25 years. Because of its German ancestry, it lost favor during the First and Second World Wars, but today the breed is loved and cherished regardless of origin.

In 1994, the Dachshund was the eighth most commonly registered dog by the American Kennel Club.

MIND & BODY

**PHYSICAL AND BEHAVIORAL TRAITS
OF THE DACHSHUND**

The Dachshund may be a short dog, but he is tall on personality. A true hound, he knows how to use his nose to find himself the best goodies, as well as the most interesting paths to explore and the most comfortable and safe laps to settle into. He gives his all to what he loves, and if you're a true friend in his eyes, you will be rewarded with a

Facing page: There's a size and a style of Dachshund to suit everyone. This is a red standard longhaired dog.

10

gregarious yet gracious companion for life.

CONFORMATION AND PHYSICAL CHARACTERISTICS

This is not a book about show dogs, so information here will not deal with the conformation of champions and how to select one. The purpose of this chapter is to provide basic information about the stature of a Dachshund and qualities of a physical nature.

Clearly, beauty is in the eye of the beholder. And, since standards come and standards go, measuring your dog against some imaginary yardstick does little for you or your dog. Just because your dog isn't a show champion, doesn't mean that he or she is any less of a family member. And, just because a dog is a champion doesn't mean that he or she is not a genetic time bomb waiting to go off.

When breeders and those interested in showing Dachshunds are selecting dogs, they are looking for those qualities that match the breed "standard." This standard, however, is of an imaginary Dachshund, and it changes from time to time and from country to country. Thus, the conformation and physical characteristics that pet owners should concentrate on are somewhat different and much more practical.

Dachshunds are a chondrodystrophoid breed, which is why they have short legs. The elongated body is also part of their genetics, and it makes them prone to intervertebral disk disease. In fact, the Dachshund has the highest incidence for this disease of any breed. Because of this, there are some precautions that would seem prudent. When lifting your Dachshund, support the chest from underneath with your arm and lift the dog horizontally so as not to stress the spine. For the same reasons, do not encourage your Dachshund to jump. This breed was designed for moving quickly and efficiently on a horizontal, not vertical, plane.

The Dachshund comes in two sizes. Miniature Dachshunds are

The Dachshund's long, narrow physique enables him to fit into narrow burrows.

The most popular coat type is smooth, like these puppies. It was also the first type to be registered by the American Kennel Club.

under 10 pounds in weight after one year of age and Standard Dachshunds weigh more than this, generally from 18–25 pounds. Since the Dachshund sometimes has a tendency towards obesity, this optimal limit may be exceeded by pets. In other countries there tends to be more variability. For example, in Germany, the dogs are identified as either Standard, Miniature, or Kaninchenteckel, based on chest measurements taken at fifteen months of age. The circumference of the chest is used because the smaller varieties (Kaninchenteckel and Zwergteckel) need to be able to fit into a narrow rabbit burrow.

COAT COLOR, CARE AND CONDITION

There are three varieties of coats which go with each size of Dachshund: smooth, longhaired, and wirehaired. The American Kennel Club first registered smooths in 1885. Longhaired and Wirehaired Dachshunds were not registered until 1931.

The coat variations in Dachshunds were the result of outbreeding. The smooth Dachshund is the most common, having short, smooth and shiny fur. Occasionally smooth Dachshunds produced pups with longer fur. This was the likely origin for the longhaired vari-

13

ety. Another theory suggests the longhaired Dachshund originated by outcrossing the smooth Dachshund with the various German spaniels, but that seems difficult to comprehend in people breeding "badger dogs." The wirehaired Dachshunds may have been part of the ancestral line, while some have suggested that they originated by outcrossing the smooth Dachshund with various hard-coated terriers (such as Scotch Terriers and Dandie Dinmont Terriers), schnauzers and wirehaired pinschers. Considering their relatively recent vintage, there are still many questions in Dachshund genealogy.

The Dachshund comes in a variety of colors, including red (tan), brindle, black, chocolate, gray, blue, dappled and white with tan markings. The smooth and wirehaired varieties require very little in the way of grooming. They are fairly low maintenance, requiring only routine brushing and the occasional bath. The longhaired varieties need more attention, and it is important that they be thoroughly brushed before being bathed or they will develop mats.

Coat color and texture are sometimes associated with health concerns. For example, a variety of eye diseases are seen in Dachshunds that are homozy-

Longhaired Dachshunds have flowing, silky coats that need more attention than their smooth- or wirehaired cousins.

gous for the merle coloration (inherited merle gene from each parent). Deafness is more common in the dappled Dachshund. Color dilution alopecia is seen in blue Dachshunds and eventually causes significant hair loss and scaling. Longhaired Dachshunds have a much higher incidence of undershot jaw (brachygnathism).

BEHAVIOR AND PERSONALITY OF THE ACTIVE DACHSHUND

Behavior and personality are two qualities which are hard to standardize within a breed. Although generalizations are difficult to make, most Dachshunds are alert and people-oriented. The Dachshund is known for its playfulness, individualism, energy level and determination. It is a versatile breed that can compete in several different categories. These include conformation, showing, obedience trials, field trials and earthdog trials. Dachshunds make great working dogs because they do have the capacity to be loyal, determined, watchful and obedient. However, it is their social nature that makes them want to work with people.

Behavior and personality are incredibly important in dogs, and there seems to be quite evident extremes in the Dachshund.

Dachshunds like to use their noses, but they are ultimately very social animals who love being with people.

The ideal Dachshund is neither aggressive nor neurotic but rather a loving family member with good self-esteem and acceptance of position in the family "pack." Because the Dachshund has the potential to be unruly, it is worth spending the time when selecting a pup to pay attention to any evidence of personality problems. It is also imperative that *all* Dachshunds be obedience trained. Like any dog, they have the potential to be vicious without appropriate training; consider obedience classes mandatory for your sake and that of your dog. Although it is impossible to generalize, many Dachshund owners admit that they sometimes have difficulty completely housebreaking their pet. It is not unusual for them to have the occasional "accident" in the house.

Although many Dachshunds are happy to sleep the day away in bed or on a sofa, most enjoy having a purpose in their day and that makes them excellent working dogs. Remember, they were originally bred to be hunters. They do not need long daily walks, but they do appreciate events that involve family members. All Dachshunds should attend obedience classes and they need to learn limits to unacceptable behaviors. A well-loved and well-controlled Dachshund is certain to be a valued family member.

For pet owners, there are several activities to which your Dachshund is well-suited. They make great walking and exploring companions. In fact, they tend to shadow their owners wherever they go. The loyal and loving Dachshund will also be your personal guard dog if properly trained; aggressiveness and viciousness do not fit into the equation. Dachshunds have a bark that belies a hunter's spirit within a small body.

For Dachshund enthusiasts who want to get into more competitive aspects of the dog world, showing, hunting, obedience, tracking and den trials are all activities that can be considered.

As a Dachshund owner, you might want to enjoy such activities as obedience, tracking or earthdog trials with your dog.

The loyal and loving Dachshund will be happy to accompany you anywhere, outdoors or in.

SELECTING

**WHAT YOU NEED TO KNOW TO FIND
THE BEST DACHSHUND PUPPY**

Owning the perfect Dachshund rarely happens by accident. On the other hand, owning a genetic dud is almost always the result of an impulse purchase and failure to do even basic research. Buying this book is a major step in understanding the situation and making intelligent choices.

**Facing page:
Before you fall in
love with an
irresistible puppy,
do some research
so you know
you're getting a
well-bred, healthy
animal.**

SOURCES

Recently, a large survey was done to determine whether there were more problems seen in animals adopted from pet stores, breeders, private owners or animal shelters. Somewhat surprisingly, there didn't appear to be any major difference in total number of problems seen from these sources. What was different were the kinds of problems seen in each source. Thus, you can't rely on any one source because there are no standards by which judgments can be made. Most veterinarians will recommend that you select a "good breeder," but there is no way to identify such an individual. A breeder of champion show dogs may also be a breeder of genetic defects.

The best approach is to select a pup from a source that regularly performs genetic screening and has documentation to prove it. If you are intending to be a pet owner, don't worry about whether your pup is show quality. A mark here or there that might disqualify the pup as a show winner has absolutely no impact on its ability to be a loving and healthy pet. Also, the vast majority of dogs will be neutered and not used for breeding anyway. Concentrate on the things that are important.

MEDICAL SCREENING

Whether you are dealing with a breeder, a breed rescue group, a shelter or a pet store, your approach should be the same. You want to identify a Dachshund that you can live with and screen it for medical and behavioral problems before you make it a permanent family member. If the source you select has not done the important testing needed, make sure they will offer you a health/temperament guarantee before you remove the dog from the premises to have the work done yourself. If this is not acceptable, or they are offering an exchange-only policy, keep moving; this isn't

It's a good idea to see the mother and, if possible, the father of the puppy you want; chances are the puppy will be a lot like them!

the right place for you to get a dog. As soon as you purchase a Dachshund, pup or adult, go to your veterinarian for thorough evaluation and testing.

Pedigree analysis is best left to true enthusiasts, but there are some things that you can do, even as a novice. Inbreeding is to be discouraged so check out your four- or five-generation pedigree and look for names that appear repeatedly. Reputable breeders will usually not allow inbreeding at least three generations back in the puppy's pedigree. Also ask the breeder to provide OFA and CERF registration numbers on all ancestors in the pedigree for which testing is done. If there are a lot of gaps, the breeder has some explaining to do.

The screening procedure is easier if you select an older dog. Animals can be registered for hips and elbows as young as two years of age by the Orthopedic Foundation for Animals and by one year of age by Genetic Disease Control. This is your insurance against hip dysplasia and elbow dysplasia later in life. Although Dachshunds now have a relatively low incidence of these orthopedic problems, it is because of the efforts of conscientious breeders who have been doing the appropriate testing. A verbal testimonial that they've never heard of the condition in their lines is not adequate and probably means they really don't know if they have a problem. Move along.

Evaluation is somewhat more complicated in the Dachshund puppy. The PennHip™ procedure can determine risk for developing hip dysplasia in pups as young as 16 weeks of age. For pups younger than that, you should request copies of OFA or GDC registration for both parents. If the parents haven't both been registered, their hip and elbow status should be considered unknown and questionable.

All Dachshunds, regardless of age, should be screened for evidence of von Willebrand's disease. This can be accomplished with a simple blood test. The incidence is high enough in the breed that there is no excuse for not performing the test.

For animals older than one year of age, your veterinarian will also want to take a blood sample to check for thyroid function in addition to von Willebrand's disease. Both are common in the Dachshund. A heartworm test, urinalysis and evaluation of feces for internal parasites is also indicated. The urinalysis is to detect evidence of urinary tract infection and

As puppies grow, they can be screened for a number of diseases, as well as for temperament.

stones since the breed is so prone to cystinuria. If there are any patches of hair loss, a skin scraping should be taken to determine if the dog has evidence of demodectic mange.

Your veterinarian should also perform a very thorough ophthalmologic (eye) examination. The most common eye problems in Dachshunds are cataracts, persistent pupillary membranes and retinal dysplasia. It is best to acquire a pup whose parents have both been screened for heritable eye diseases and certified "clear" by organizations such as CERF. If this has been the case, an examination by your veterinarian is probably sufficient and referral to an ophthalmologist is only necessary if recommended by your veterinarian.

BEHAVIORAL SCREENING

Medical screening is important but don't forget temperament. More dogs are killed each year for behavioral reasons than for all medical problems combined. Temperament testing is a valuable although not infallible tool in the screening process. The reason that temperament is so important is that many dogs are eventually destroyed because they exhibit undesirable behaviors. Although not all behaviors are evident in young pups (e.g., aggression often takes many months to manifest itself), detecting anxious and fearful pups (and avoiding them) can be very important in the selection process. Traits most identifiable in the young pup include: fear; excitability; low pain threshold; extreme submission; and noise sensitivity. There are many different techniques available and a complete discussion is beyond the scope of this book. References are provided to encourage you to investigate further.

Pups can be evaluated for temperament as early as 7—8 weeks of age. Some behaviorists, breeders and trainers recommend objective testing where scores are given in several different categories. Others are more casual about the process since it is only a crude indicator anyway. In general, the evaluation takes place in three stages, by someone the pup has not been exposed to. The testing is not done within 72 hours of vaccination or surgery. First, the pup is observed and handled to determine its sociability. Puppies with obvious undesirable traits such as shyness, hyperactivity or uncontrollable biting may turn out to be unsuitable. Second, the desired pup is separated from the others and then observed for how they respond when played with and called. Third, the pup should be stimulated in various ways and their responses noted. Suitable activities include lying the pup on its side, grooming it, clipping its nails, gently grasping it around the muzzle and testing its reactions to noise. In a study conducted at the Psychology Department of Colorado State University, the researchers also found that heart rate was a

Greeting another dog in a friendly way is a sign of a stable temperament.

A puppy aptitude test can help an owner determine how confident his puppy is in certain situations. This is Michael Kirkpatrick's puppy, Red Baron.

good indicator in this third stage of evaluation. Actually, they noted the resting heart rates, stimulated the pups with a loud noise and measured how long it took the heart rates to recover to resting levels. Most pups recovered within 36 seconds. Dogs that took considerably longer were more likely to be anxious.

Puppy aptitude tests (PAT) can be given in which a numerical score is given for eleven different traits, with a "1" representing the most assertive or aggressive expression of a trait and a "6" representing disinterest, independence or inaction. The traits assessed in the PAT include: social attraction to people; following; restraint; social dominance; elevation (lifting off

ground by evaluator); retrieve; touch sensitivity; sound sensitivity; prey/chase drive; stability; and energy level. Although the tests do not absolutely predict behaviors, they do tend to do well at predicting puppies at behavioral extremes.

ORGANIZATIONS YOU SHOULD KNOW ABOUT

Project TEACH™ (Training and Education in Animal Care and Health) is a voluntary accreditation process for those individuals selling animals to the public. It is administered by Pet Health Initiative, Inc. (PHI) and provides instruction on genetic screening as well as many other aspects of proper pet care. TEACH-accredited sources screen animals for a variety of medical, behavioral and infectious diseases *before* they are sold. Project TEACH™ supports the efforts of registries such as OFA, GDC and CERF and recommends that all animals sold be registered with the appropriate agencies. For more information on Project TEACH™, send a self-addressed stamped envelope to Pet Health Initiative, P.O. Box 12093, Scottsdale, AZ 85267-2093.

The Orthopedic Foundation for Animals (OFA) is a nonprofit organization established in 1966

The Orthopedic Foundation for Animals (OFA) tests dogs for diseases like hip and elbow dysplasia.

So that dogs can live full lives as city or country companions, they should be tested early for potential problems.

to collect and disseminate information concerning orthopedic diseases of animals and to establish control programs to lower the incidence of orthopedic diseases in animals. A registry is maintained for both hip dysplasia and elbow dysplasia. The ultimate purpose of OFA certification is to provide information to dog owners to assist in the selection of good breeding animals; therefore, attempts to get a dysplastic dog certified will only hurt the breed by perpetuation of the disease. For more information contact your veterinarian or the Orthopedic Foundation for Animals, 2300 Nifong Blvd., Columbia, MO 65201.

The Institute for Genetic Disease Control in Animals (GDC) is a nonprofit organization founded in 1990 and maintains an open registry for orthopedic problems but does not compete with OFA. In an open registry like GDC, owners, breeders, veterinarians, and scientists can trace the genetic history of any particular dog once that dog and close relatives have been registered. At the present time, the GDC operates Open Registries for hip dysplasia, elbow dysplasia, and osteochondrosis. The GDC is currently developing guidelines for registries of Legg-Calve-Perthes disease, cranio-mandibular osteopathy, and medial patellar luxation. Of these, Legg-Calve-Perthes disease and medial patellar luxation are significant in the Dachshund. For more information, contact the Institute for Genetic Disease Control in Animals, P.O. Box 222, Davis, CA 95617.

The Canine Eye Registration Foundation (CERF) is an international organization devoted to eliminating hereditary eye diseases from purebred dogs. This organization is similar to OFA, which helps eliminate disease like hip dysplasia. CERF is a non-profit organization that screens and certifies purebreds as free of heritable eye diseases. Dogs are evaluated by veterinary eye specialists and finding are then submitted to CERF for documentation. The goal is to identify purebreds without heritable eye problems so they can be used for breeding. Dogs being considered for breeding programs should be screened and certified by CERF on an annual basis since not all problems are evident in puppies. For more information on CERF, write to CERF, SCC-A, Purdue University, West Lafayette, IN 47907.

The Canine Eye Registration Foundation (CERF) tests dogs for heritable eye diseases.

FEEDING &
NUTRITION

**WHAT YOU NEED TO CONSIDER EVERY DAY TO FEED YOUR
DACHSHUND THROUGH HIS LIFETIME**

Nutrition is one of the most important aspects of raising a healthy Dachshund, and yet it is often the source of much controversy between breeders, veterinarians, pet owners and dog food manufacturers. However, most of these arguments have more to do with marketing than with science.

Facing page: Healthy dogs have healthy appetites, and should be fed a high-quality commercial dog food.

Let's first take a look at dog foods and then determine the needs of our dog. This chapter will concentrate on feeding the pet Dachshund rather than breeding or working animals.

COMMERCIAL DOG FOODS

Most dog foods are sold based on marketing (i.e., how to make a product appealing to owners while meeting the needs of dogs). Some foods are marketed on the basis of their protein content, others based on a "special" ingredient and some are sold because they don't contain certain ingredients (e.g., preservatives, soy). We want a dog food that specifically meets our dog's needs, is economical and causes few if any problems. Most foods come in dry, semi-moist and canned forms. Some can now be purchased frozen. The "dry" foods are the most economical, and contain the least fat and the most preservatives. The canned foods are the most expensive (they're 75% water), usually contain the most fat, and have the least preservatives. Semi-moist foods are expensive, high in sugar content and I do not recommend them for any dogs.

When you're selecting a commercial diet, make sure the food has been assessed by feeding trials for a specific life stage, not just by nutrient analysis. This statement is usually located not far from the ingredient label. In the United States, these trials are performed in accordance with American Association of Feed Control Officials (AAFCO), and in Canada by the Canadian Veterinary Medical Association. This certification is important because it has been found that dog foods currently on the market that provide only a chemical analysis and calculated values but no feeding trial may not provide adequate nutrition. The feeding trials show that the diets meet minimal, not optimal, standards. However, they are the best tests we currently have.

PUPPY REQUIREMENTS

Soon after pups are born, and certainly within the first 24 hours, they should begin nursing their mother. This provides them with colostrum, which is an antibody-rich milk that helps protect them from infection for their first few months of life. Pups should be allowed to nurse for at least six weeks before they are completely weaned from their mother. Supplemental feeding may be started by as early as three weeks of age.

By two months of age, pups should be fed puppy food. They

are now in an important growth phase. Nutritional deficiencies and/or imbalances during this time of life are more devastating than at any other time. Also, this is not the time to overfeed pups or provide them with "performance" rations. Overfeeding Dachshunds is not advised because they have a tendency towards obesity and because it can put additional stress on intervertebral disks.

Pups should be fed "growth" diets until they are 9—12 months of age. Pups will initially need to be fed 2—3 meals daily until they are 12 months old, then once to twice daily (preferably twice) when they are converted to adult food. Puppy diets tend to be higher in calories than maintenance diets, so veterinarians often like to convert the obesity-prone Dachshund to the lower-calorie diet by one year of age at the latest. Proper growth diets should be selected based on acceptable feeding trials designed for growing pups. If you can't tell by reading the label, ask your veterinarian for feeding advice.

Remember that pups need "balance" in their diets, and avoid the temptation to supplement with protein, vitamins, or minerals. Calcium supplements have been implicated as a cause of bone and cartilage deformity, especially in large-breed puppies. Puppy diets are already heavily fortified with calcium, and supplements tend to unbalance the mineral intake. There is more than adequate proof that these supplements are responsible for many bone deformities seen in these growing dogs.

Puppies get colostrum-rich milk from their mothers when they first start nursing.

ADULT DIETS

The goal of feeding adult dogs is one of "maintenance." They have already done the growing they are going to do and are unlikely to have the digestive problems of elderly dogs. In general, dogs can do well on maintenance rations containing predominantly plant or animal-based ingredients as long as that ration has been specifically formulated to meet maintenance level requirements. This contention should be supported by studies performed by the manufacturer in accordance with AAFCO

An energetic, growing youngster has a higher calorie requirement than his more sedate parent.

(American Association of Feed Control Officials). In Canada, these products should be certified by the Canadian Veterinary Medical Association to meet maintenance requirements.

There's nothing wrong with feeding a cereal-based diet to dogs on maintenance rations and they are the most economical. In fact, many Dachshunds do better on diets that provide most of their amino acids as plant protein rather than meat. This is because some Dachshunds have a metabolic disease that causes them to lose the amino acid cystine in their urine and this can result in kidneys stones. The "stones" are more likely to dissolve and not cause problems in alkaline urine and meat diets tend to make the urine more acidic (which promotes stone formation).

When comparing maintenance rations, it must be appreciated that these diets must meet the "minimum" requirements for confined dogs, not necessarily optimal levels. Most dogs will benefit when fed diets that contain easily digested ingredients that provide nutrients at least slightly above minimum requirements. Typically, these foods will be intermediate in price between the most expensive super-premium diets and the cheapest generic diets. Select only those diets that have been substantiated by feeding trials to meet maintenance requirements, those that contain wholesome ingredients, and those recommended by your veterinarian. Don't select based on price alone, on company advertising, or on total protein content.

GERIATRIC DIETS

Dachshunds are considered elderly when they are about seven years of age, and there are certain changes that occur as dogs age that alter their nutritional requirements. As pets age, their metabolism slows and this must be accounted for. If maintenance rations are fed in the same amounts while metabolism is slowing, weight gain may result. Obesity is the last thing one wants to contend with in an elderly pet, since it increases their risk of several other health-related problems. As pets age, most of their organs function not as well as in youth. The digestive system, the liver, pancreas and gallbladder are not functioning at peak effect. The intestines have more difficulty extracting all the nutrients from the food consumed. A gradual decline in kidney function is considered a normal part of aging.

A responsible approach to geriatric nutrition is to realize that degenerative changes are a normal part of aging. Our goal is to minimize the potential damage done by taking this into account while the dog is still well. If we wait until an elderly dog is ill before we change the diet, we have a much harder job.

Elderly dogs need to be treated as individuals. While some benefit from the nutrition found in "senior" diets, others might do better on the highly digestible puppy and super-premium diets. These latter diets provide an excellent blend of digestibility and amino acid content but, unfortunately, many are higher in salt and phosphorus than the older pet really needs.

Older dogs are also more prone to developing arthritis; therefore, it is important not to overfeed them, since obesity puts added stress on the joints. For animals with joint pain, supplementing the diet with fatty acid combinations containing cis-linoleic acid, gamma-linolenic acid and eicosapentaenoic acid can be quite beneficial.

MEDICAL CONDITIONS AND DIET

Obesity is the most common nutritional disease afflicting dogs and cats today, currently exceeding all deficiency related diseases combined. It is extremely common in the Dachshund. Perhaps the pet food companies have done their jobs too well, but the newer foods are probably much tastier to pets than previous ones and encourage eating. Because many people leave food down all day for free-choice feeding, animals consume more and gain weight.

The incidence of obesity increases with age. It is about twice as common in neutered as in nonneutered animals of either sex and, up to 12 years of age, is more common in females than in males. Recent studies indicate that even moderate obesity can significantly reduce both the quality and the length of an animal's life. Fortunately, it is a situation that can be remedied.

Neutered animals should be fed a nutritionally balanced, reduced-calorie diet that has been specifically formulated for the high-risk, obesity-prone animal. Weight reduction in most animals can be accomplished with a medically supervised program of caloric restriction. This requires the genuine, long-term commitment by the pet owner to alter poor feeding habits and provide adequate exercise.

It is important to keep in mind that dietary choices can affect the development of orthopedic diseases such as hip dysplasia, osteochondrosis and perhaps intervertebral disk disease. When feeding a pup at risk, avoid high-calorie diets and try to feed several times a day rather than ad libitum. Also avoid supplements of calcium, phosphorus and vitamin D as they can interfere with normal bone and cartilage development. The fact is that calcium levels in the body are carefully regulated by hormones (such as calcitonin and parathormone) as well as vitamin D. Supplementation disturbs this normal regulation and can cause many problems. If you really feel the need to supplement your dog, select products

A proper diet is critical to the formation and maintenance of strong bones, a shiny coat and a normal activity level. Paz, owned by Karyn Villarreal, poses on an agility course obstacle.

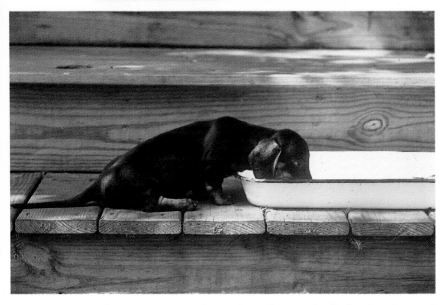

Growing puppies need several meals a day and all the fresh, cool water they can drink.

such as eicosapentaenoic/gamma-linolenic fatty acid combinations or small amounts of vitamin C.

Fat supplements are probably the most common supplements purchased from pet supply stores. They frequently promise to add luster, gloss, and sheen to the coat, and consequently make dogs look healthy. The only fatty acid that is essential for this purpose is cis-linoleic acid, which is found in flaxseed oil, sunflower seed oil, and safflower oil. Corn oil is a suitable but less effective alternative. Most of the other oils found in retail supplements are high in saturated and monounsaturated fats and are not beneficial for shiny fur or

healthy skin. For dogs with allergies, arthritis, high blood pressure (hypertension), high cholesterol, and some heart ailments, other fatty acids may be prescribed by a veterinarian. The important ingredients in these products are gamma-linolenic acid (GLA), eicosapentaenoic acid (EPA), and docosahexaenoic acid (DHA). These products have gentle and natural anti-inflammatory properties. But don't be fooled by imitations. Most retail fatty acid supplements do not contain these functional forms of the essential fatty acids—look for gamma-linolenic acid, eicosapentaenoic acid, and docosahexaenoic acid on the label.

HEALTH

PREVENTIVE MEDICINE AND HEALTH CARE FOR YOUR DACHSHUND

Keeping your Dachshund healthy requires preventive health care. This is not only the most effective, but the least expensive way to battle illness. Good preventive care starts even before puppies are born. The dam should be well cared for, vaccinated and free of infections and parasites.

Facing page: Regular visits to the veterinarian are a sure way to keep your Dachshund healthy.

36

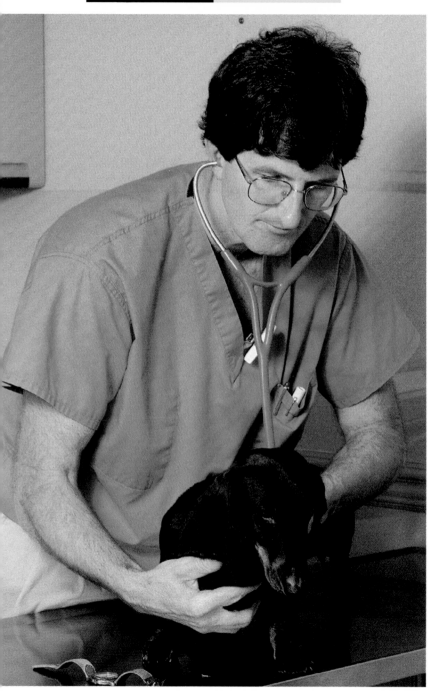

Hopefully, both parents were screened for important genetic diseases (e.g. von Willebrands's disease), registered with the appropriate agencies (e.g., OFA, GDC, CERF), showed no evidence of medical or behavioral problems and were found to be good candidates for breeding. This gives the pup a good start in life. If all has been planned well, the dam will pass on resistance to disease to her pups that will last for the first few months of life. However, the dam can also pass on parasites, infections, genetic diseases and more.

TWO TO THREE WEEKS OF AGE

By two to three weeks of life, it is usually necessary to start pups on a regimen to control worms. Although dogs benefit from this parasite control, the primary reason for doing this is human health. After whelping, the dam often sheds large numbers of worms even if she tested negative previously. This is because many worms lay dormant in tissues and the stress of delivery causes parasite release and shedding into the environment. Assume that all puppies potentially have worms because studies have shown that 75% do. Thus, we institute worm control early to protect the people in the house

from worms, more than the pups themselves. The deworming is repeated every two to three weeks until your veterinarian feels the condition is under control. Nursing bitches should be treated at the same time because they often shed worms during this time. Only use products recommended by your veterinarian. Over-the-counter parasiticides have been responsible for deaths in pups.

Puppies need a series of shots before they're six months old, but even adults need regular vaccines.

SIX TO TWENTY WEEKS OF AGE

Most puppies are weaned from their mother at 6–8 weeks of age. Weaning shouldn't be done too early so that pups have the opportunity to socialize with their littermates and dam. This is important for them to be able to respond to other dogs later in life. There is no reason to rush the weaning process unless the dam can't produce enough milk to feed the pups.

Pups are usually first examined by their veterinarian at six to eight weeks of age which is when most vaccination schedules commence. If pups are exposed to many other dogs at this young age, veterinarians often opt for vaccinating with inactivated parvovirus at six weeks of age. When exposure isn't a factor, most veterinarians would rather wait to see the pup at eight weeks of age. At this point, they can also do a preliminary dental evaluation to see that all the puppy teeth are coming in

correctly, check to see that the testicles are properly descending in males and that there are no health reasons to prohibit vaccination at this time. Heart murmurs, wandering knee-caps (luxating patellae), juvenile cataracts, persistent pupillary membranes (a congenital eye disease), brachygnathism (undershot jaw) and hernias are usually evident by this time.

Your veterinarian may also be able to perform temperament testing on the pup by eight weeks of age, or recommend someone to do it for you. Although temperament testing is not completely accurate, it can often predict which pups are most anxious and fearful. Some form of temperament evaluation is im-

After eight weeks of age, your veterinarian can check your puppy for a number of things, including heart murmurs, hernias and an undershot bite.

portant because behavioral problems account for more animals being euthanized (killed) each year than all medical conditions combined.

Recently, some veterinary hospitals have been recommending neutering pups as early as six to eight weeks of age. A study done at the University of Florida College of Veterinary Medicine over a span of more than four years concluded there was no increase in complications when animals were neutered when less than six months of age. The evaluators also concluded that the surgery appeared to be less stressful when done in young pups.

Most vaccination schedules consist of injections being given at 6–8, 10–12 and 14–16 weeks of age. Ideally, vaccines should not be given closer than two weeks apart and three to four weeks seems to be optimal. Each vaccine usually consists of several different viruses (e.g., parvovirus, distemper, parainfluenza, hepatitis) combined into one injection. Coronavirus can be given as a separate vaccination according to this same schedule if pups are at risk. Some veterinarians and breeders advise another parvovirus booster at 18–20 weeks of age. A booster is given for all vaccines at one year of age and annually thereafter. For animals at increased risk of exposure, parvovirus vaccination may be given as often as four times a year. A new vaccine for canine cough (tracheobronchitis) is squirted into the nostrils. It can be given as early as six weeks of age if pups are at risk. Leptospirosis vaccination is given in some geographic areas and likely offers protection for six to eight months. The initial series consists of three to four injections spaced two to three weeks apart, starting as early as ten weeks of age. Rabies vaccine is given as a separate injection at three months of age, then repeated when the pup is one year old, then every one to three years depending on local risk and government regulation.

Some dogs have difficulty mounting a complete and protective response to vaccinations. In the Dachshund, the most likely reason for this is combined immunodeficiency, which is inherited as a sex-linked recessive trait. That means that females carry the trait but that it most often causes problems in males. Your veterinarian can test antibody levels if he suspects an immune problem in a pup. In these cases, we typically also recommend running a test to measure antibody titer (level) for parvovirus at 16 weeks of age and annually thereafter. This helps ensure that the vaccinations that are given will, in fact, be protective.

Between eight and fourteen weeks of age, use every opportunity to expose the pup to as many people and situations as possible. This is part of the critical socialization period that will determine how good a pet your dog will become. This is not the time to abandon a puppy for eight hours while you go to work. This is also not the time to punish your dog in any way, shape or form.

This is the time to introduce your dog to neighborhood cats, birds and other creatures. Hold off on exposure to other dogs until after the second vaccination in the series. You don't want your new friend to pick up contagious diseases from dogs it meets in its travels before it has adequate protection. By twelve weeks of age, your pup should be ready for social outings with other dogs. Do them—they're a great way for your dog to feel comfortable around members of its own species. Walk the streets and introduce your pup to everybody you meet. Your goal should be to introduce your dog to every type of person or situation it is likely to encounter in its

Puppies should be introduced to all kinds of people at a young age so they are not afraid of anyone as adults.

life. Take it in cars, elevators, buses, travel crates, subways, parade grounds, beaches; you want it to habituate to all environments. Expose your pup to kids, teenagers, old people, people in wheelchairs, people on bicycles, people in uniforms. The more varied the exposure, the better the socialization.

Proper identification of your pet is also important since this minimizes the risk of theft and increases the chances that your pet will be returned to you if it is lost. There are several different options. Microchip implantation is a relatively painless procedure involving the subcutaneous injection of an implant the size of a grain of rice. This implant does not act as a beacon if your pet goes missing. However, if your pet turns up at a veterinary clinic or shelter and is checked with a scanner, the chip provides information about the owner that can be used to quickly reunite you with your pet. This method of identification is reasonably priced, permanent in nature, and performed at most veterinary clinics. Another option is tattooing which can be done on the inner ear or on the skin of the abdomen. Most purebreds are given a number by the associated registry (e.g., American Kennel Club, United Kennel Club, Canadian Kennel Club, etc.) and this is used for identification. Alternatively, permanent numbers such as social security numbers (telephone numbers and addresses may change during the life of your pet) can be used in the tattooing process. There are several different tattoo registries maintaining lists of dogs, their tattoo codes and their owners. Finally, identifying collars and tags provide quick information but can be separated from your pet if it is lost or stolen. They work best when combined with a permanent identification system such as microchip implantation or tattooing.

FOUR TO TWELVE MONTHS OF AGE

At 16 weeks of age, when your pup gets the last in its series of regular induction vaccinations, ask your veterinarian about evaluating the pup for hip dysplasia with the PennHip™ technique. This helps predict the risk of developing hip dysplasia as well as degenerative joint disease. Dachshund breeders have been very successful in decreasing the incidence of hip dysplasia through routine screening and registration programs. Since anesthesia is typically required for the procedure, many veterinarians like to do the evaluation at the same time as neutering.

At this same time, it is very worthwhile to perform a diagnostic test for von Willebrand's disease, an inherited disorder that causes uncontrolled bleeding. This trait is relatively common in the Dachshund. A simple blood test is all that is required, but it may need to be sent to a special laboratory to have the test performed. You will be extremely happy you had the foresight to have this done before neutering. If your dog does have a bleeding problem, it will be necessary to take special precautions during surgery.

Also when your pet is six months of age, your veterinarian will want to take a blood sample to perform a heartworm test. If the test is negative and shows no evidence of heartworm infection, the pup will go on heartworm prevention therapy. Some veterinarians are even recommending preventive therapy in younger pups. This might be a one-a-day regimen, but newer therapies can be given on a once-a-month basis. As a bonus, most of these heartworm preventatives also help prevent internal parasites (worms, as mentioned above).

The six-month checkup is also a good time to have a urine sample analyzed. Dachshunds have a high incidence of the metabolic disease cystinuria in which they lose the amino acid cystine into the urine. In some cases, this results in kidney stones that can have serious consequences. A simple urine test can be assessed for pH (stones tend to form more in acidic urine), bacteria (infection is commonly associated with the condition) and even cystine levels if your veterinarian feels that it is warranted. If your pet does have cystinuria, your veterinarian will likely want to effect a dietary change before further problems are noted.

As a general rule, neuter your animal at about 6 months of age unless you fully intend to breed it. As mentioned earlier, neutering can be safely done at eight weeks of age but this is still not a common practice. Neutering not only stops the possibility of pregnancy and undesirable behaviors, but can prevent several health problems as well. It is a well established fact that pups spayed before their first heat have a dramatically reduced incidence of mammary (breast) cancer. Neutered males significantly decrease their incidence of prostate disorders.

If your Dachshund has any patches of hair loss, your veterinarian will want to perform a skin scraping with a scalpel blade to see if any *Demodex* mites are responsible. If there is a problem, don't lose hope; about 90% of demodicosis cases can be cured with supportive care only. However, it's important to diagnose it early before scarring results.

Another part of the sixth-month visit should be a thorough dental evaluation to make sure all the permanent teeth have correctly erupted. If they haven't, this will be the time to correct the problem. Correction should only be performed to make the animal more comfort-

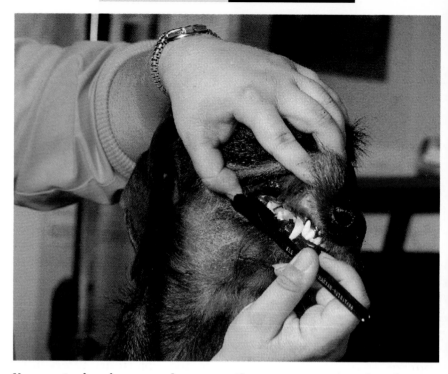

Your veterinarian can show you the correct way to brush your Dachshund's teeth to prevent plaque and tartar build-up.

able and promote more normal chewing. The procedures should never be used to cosmetically improve the appearance of a dog used for show purposes or breeding.

After the dental evaluation, you should start implementing home dental care. In most cases, this will consist of brushing the teeth one or more times each week and perhaps using dental rinses. It is a sad fact that 85% of dogs over four years of age have periodontal disease and doggy breath. In fact it is so common that most people think it is "normal." Well, it is normal—as normal as bad breath would be in people if they never brushed their teeth. Brush your dog's teeth regularly with a special tooth brush and toothpaste and you can greatly reduce the incidence of tartar buildup, bad breath and gum disease. Better preventive care means that dogs live a long time. They'll enjoy their sunset years more if they still have their teeth. Ask your veterinarian for details on home dental care.

THE FIRST SEVEN YEARS

At one year of age, your dog should be re-examined and have boosters for all vaccines. Your veterinarian will also want to do a very thorough physical examination to look for early evidence of problems. This might include taking radiographs (x-rays) of the hips and elbows to look for evidence of dysplastic changes. Genetic Disease Control (GDC) will certify hips and elbows at 12 months of age; Orthopedic Foundation for Animals won't issue certification until 24 months of age.

At 12 months of age, it's also a great time to have some blood samples analyzed to provide background information. Al-though few Dachshunds experience clinical hypothyroidism at this young age, the process may be starting. Therefore, it is a good idea to have baseline levels of thyroid hormones (free and total), TSH (thyroid-stimulating hormone), blood cell counts, organ chemistries, and cholesterol levels. This can serve as a valuable comparison to samples collected in the future.

Each year, preferably around the time of your pet's birthday, it's time for another veterinary visit. This visit is a wonderful opportunity for a thorough clinical examination rather than just "shots." Since 85% of dogs have periodontal disease by four years of age, veterinary intervention

The Roar-Hide™ is a safe chew toy that keeps dogs happy and occupied while strengthening their teeth and gums.

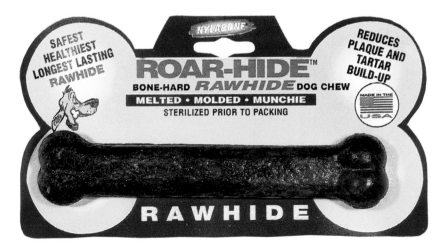

does not seem to be as wide-spread as it should be. The examination should include visually inspecting the ears, eyes (a great time to start scrutinizing for progressive retinal atrophy, cataracts, etc.), mouth (don't wait for gum disease), and groin, listening (auscultation) to the lungs and heart, feeling (palpating) the lymph nodes and abdomen and answering all of your questions about optimal health care. In addition, booster vaccinations are given during these times, feces are checked for parasites, urine is analyzed and blood samples may be col-lected for analysis. One of the tests run on the blood sample is for heartworm antigen. In areas of the country where heartworm is only present in the spring, summer and fall (it's spread by mosquitoes), blood samples are collected and evaluated about a month prior to the mosquito season. Other routine blood tests are for blood cells (hematology), organ chemistries, thyroid levels and electrolytes.

By two years of age, most veterinarians prefer to begin preventive dental cleanings, often referred to as "prophies." Anesthesia is required and the veteri-

Heartworm is spread by infected mosquitoes, so if your puppy spends any time outdoors, he will need to be tested and put on a heartworm preventative medication.

These senior Dachshunds are proof that dogs can live long and healthy lives with proper care.

narian or veterinary dentist will use an ultrasonic scaler to remove plaque and tartar from above and below the gum line and polish the teeth so that plaque has a harder time sticking to the teeth. Radiographs (x-rays) and fluoride treatments are other options. It is now known that it is plaque, not tartar, that initiates inflammation in the gums. Since scaling and root planing remove more tartar than plaque, veterinary dentists have begun using a new technique called PerioBUD (Periodontal Bactericidal Ultrasonic Debridement). The ultrasonic treatment is quicker, disrupts more bacteria and is less irritating to the gums. With tooth polishing to finish up the procedure, gum healing is better and owners can start home care

sooner. Each dog has its own dental needs that must be addressed, but most veterinary dentists recommend prophies annually.

SENIOR DACHSHUNDS

Dachshunds are considered seniors when they reach about seven years of age. Veterinarians still usually only need to examine them once a year, but it is now important to start screening for geriatric problems.

Accordingly, blood profiles, urinalysis, chest radiographs (x-rays) and electrocardiograms (EKG) are recommended on an annual basis. When problems are caught early, they are much more likely to be successfully managed. This is as true in canine medicine as it is in human medicine.

MEDICAL PROBLEMS

RECOGNIZED GENETIC CONDITIONS SPECIFICALLY RELATED TO THE DACHSHUND

Many conditions appear to be especially prominent in Dachshunds. Sometimes it is possible to identify the genetic basis of a problem, but in many cases, we must be satisfied with merely identifying the breeds that are at risk and how the conditions can be identified, treated and prevented.

Facing page: Dachshunds are prone to a number of medical problems that your veterinarian will want to monitor.

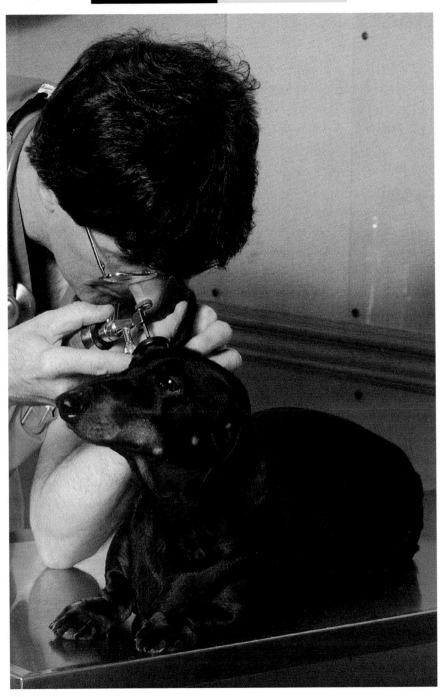

Following are some conditions that have been recognized as being common in the Dachshund but this listing is certainly not complete. Also, many genetic conditions may be common in certain breed lines, not in the breed in general.

ACANTHOSIS NIGRICANS

Acanthosis nigricans is a darkening and thickening of the skin in the armpit and groin areas. It is almost exclusively seen in the Dachshund. In time, affected dogs develop thick, dark and hairless skin on their whole underside and they become quite greasy. Diagnosis is not usually too difficult because the clinical appearance is quite characteristic. Despite the fact that acanthosis nigricans is essentially a "Dachshund disease," the precise genetics of the condition are still not certain.

There is no cure for acanthosis nigricans but there are several approaches to improving the situation. In people, acanthosis nigricans is usually associated with an internal cancer. This is not the case in dogs. Thus, treatment need not be so aggressive. Oral vitamin E and frequent use of grease-cutting shampoos often make the situation tolerable. Melatonin is also used (on an experimental basis) to lighten the pigmentation of the skin. Affected animals should not be used for breeding.

CUTANEOUS ASTHENIA

Cutaneous asthenia (Ehlers-Danlos syndrome) is a biochemical disorder that causes the skin to be overly fragile and stretchable. These animals are the rubber men of the dog world. When the skin of affected dogs is pulled, it stretches excessively to the point where it can even tear. The genetic nature of the condition is complex, but there is much evidence to suggest a dominant trend in the Dachshund.

The condition is usually easily diagnosed but if there is any question a series of measurements can be taken that consti-

A puppy's skin should be pliant and supple; however, if it's too stretchable and fragile, the Dachshund could have cutaneous asthenia.

tute a skin extensibility index. Biopsies are sometimes helpful but are not diagnostic in all cases. There is no specific treatment for cutaneous asthenia because there is no method to overcome the inherited collagen defect. Large doses of vitamin C (vitamin C is a cofactor in collagen synthesis) may be given but this will not correct the problem. These animals should definitely not be bred. Further, it is usually not safe for them to undergo surgery, even neutering.

CYSTINE UROLITHIASIS

Some Dachshunds have an inherited metabolic defect that causes them to lose the amino acid cystine in their urine. This condition is known as primary cystinuria and occurs equally in both sexes. The Dachshund is the breed most often reported with this disorder. Some of these affected dogs (predominantly males) also develop kidney stones. The exact mechanism for why some dogs develop "stones" (uroliths) while others don't is not completely known. Dogs that produce acidic urine have more problems with kidney stones probably because the cystine is more soluble in alkaline urine. Males are probably affected more often because they have a narrower urinary tract. The di-agnosis is made by evaluating the urine sediment and by radiography (x-rays). Cystine "stones" are not as clearly evident on radiographs as some others such as oxalate or struvite. The "stones" themselves can be sent to a special laboratory for analysis and confirmation.

Treatment is aimed at removing existing stones, controlling any infection and preventing the condition from recurring. Surgery is often needed to remove large or numerous uroliths; medical therapy has not been effective in dissolving cystine "stones." Antibiotics are needed if there is an associated urinary tract infection. Once the condition is no longer problematic, it is important to stop new "stones" from forming. This is attempted by altering the diet to keep the urine pH in the alkaline range or by adding sodium bicarbonate (baking soda) to the existing diet. A medication (D-penicillamine) can also be given that chelates the cystine and prevents it from being lost in the urine. Dogs affected with cystinuria should not be used for breeding.

DEMODICOSIS

Demodex mites are present on the skin of all dogs but in some animals born with a defective immune system the numbers increase and begin to cause problems. Dachshunds are usually cited as one of the most common breeds affected with this condition. Although it is thought to be genetically transmitted, the mode of transmission has never been conclusively demonstrated.

Most cases of demodicosis are seen in young pups and fully 90% of cases self-cure with little or no medical intervention by the time these dogs reach immunologic maturity at 18–36 months of age. In these cases, it is suspected that the immune system is marginally compromised and eventually matures and gets the condition under control. On the other hand, some pups (about 10% of those initially affected) do not get better and, in fact, become progressively worse. These are thought to have more severe immunologic compromise and are often labeled as having "generalized demodicosis."

The diagnosis is easily made by scraping the skin with a scalpel blade and looking at the collected debris under a microscope. The *Demodex* mites are cigar-shaped and are easily seen. What is harder to identify is the immunologic defect that allowed the condition to occur in the first place. Recent research has suggested the problem may be linked to a decrease in interleukin-2 response but the genetics is still a question.

If the cause of the immune dysfunction can be cured, the mange will resolve on its own. Likewise, if the pup outgrows its immunologic immaturity or defect, the condition will self-cure. This process can best be assisted by ensuring a healthy diet is being fed, treating for any internal parasites or other diseases, and perhaps using cleansing shampoos and nutritional supplements that help bolster the immune system. However, if the condition does not resolve on its own, or if it is getting worse despite conservative therapy, special mite-killing treatments are necessary. Amitraz is the most common dip used, but experimentally, milbemycin oxime and ivermectin given daily have shown some promising results. It must be remembered that killing the mites will not restore the immune system to normal.

Regarding prevention, it is best not to breed dogs with a history of demodicosis and dogs with generalized demodicosis should *never* be bred. Although the genetic nature of this disease has not been decisively proven, it doesn't make sense to add affected individuals to the gene pool of future generations.

ELBOW DYSPLASIA

Elbow dysplasia doesn't refer to just one disease, but rather an entire complex of disorders that affect the elbow joint. It is relatively rare in the Dachshund. Since the incidence is so low, continued registration is recommended because it should be possible to completely eliminate the condition in Dachshunds by conscientious breeding. Elbow dysplasia and osteochondrosis are disorders of young dogs, with problems usually starting between four and seven months of age. The usual manifestation is a sudden onset of lameness. In time, the continued inflammation results in arthritis in those affected joints.

Radiographs (x-rays) are taken of the elbow joints and submitted to a registry for evaluation. The Orthopedic Foundation for Animals (OFA) will assign a breed registry number to those animals with normal elbows that are over 24 months of age. Abnormal elbows are reported as Grade I to III, where Grade III elbows have well-developed degenerative joint disease (arthritis). Normal elbows on individuals 24 months or older are assigned a breed registry number and are periodically reported to parent breed clubs. Genetic Disease Control for Animals (GDC) maintains an open registry for elbow dysplasia and assigns a registry number to those individuals with normal elbows at 12 months of age or older. Only animals with "normal" elbows should be used for breeding.

EPILEPSY

Idiopathic Epilepsy is usually first seen in dogs between one and three years of age. The animals are normal between seizures. The seizures often cluster with three or four seizures occurring over a one to two day period. They also tend to be cyclic, with the clusters recurring regularly over an interval of several weeks to several months. The length of the cycle is often constant in an individual. These seizures may occur while the animal is resting. Breeding studies have shown a genetic basis for the disorder in Dachshunds.

The generalized seizure usually involves certain phases. The aura is the first phase. In this phase the animal may appear restless, fearful, abnormally affectionate or show other behavioral changes. The ictus phase, the actual seizure phase, follows the aura. Here the animal usually loses consciousness and the limbs become stiff. This is followed by paddling movements of the limbs. Crying, urination, defecation and salivation may also occur. This phase may last from seconds to minutes. The final phase is post-ictus. During this phase one may see confusion, circling, blindness or sleepiness. It may last from several minutes to a few days. There is no apparent correlation between the length of the post-ictus phase and the length or severity of the ictus phase.

The most common anti-seizure drug used in veterinary medicine is phenobarbital. It is very good at preventing seizures and has few side effects. Animals may have an increase in appetite and thirst and, occasionally, temporary weakness while becoming accustomed to the drug. It is important to periodically check the level of phenobarbitol in the blood.

This is done be taking a blood sample immediately before giving the anticonvulsant medication so the concentration of drug is measured when lowest. This blood level shows if the amount of drug given needs to be increased, decreased or remain the same.

If the seizures cannot be controlled with phenobarbital, other drugs may be added to the phenobarbital as combination therapy. Successful control of seizures doesn't always mean they stop completely. Often we must be satisfied with reducing the frequency and intensity of the seizures to a level acceptable to pet and owner.

HIP DYSPLASIA

Hip dysplasia is a genetically transmitted developmental problem of the hip joint that is common in many breeds. It is also relatively rare in the Dachshund. It should therefore be possible to completely eradicate the trait in Dachshunds through conscientious breeding. When purchasing a Dachshund pup, it is best to ensure that the parents were both registered with normal hips through one of the international registries such as the Orthopedic Foundation for Animals or Genetic Disease Control. Pups over 16 weeks of age can be tested by veterinarians trained in the PennHip™ procedure which is a way of predicting risk of developing hip dysplasia and arthritis.

HYPERADRENOCORTICISM

Hyperadrenocorticism, also known as Cushing's syndrome, results when the body produces too much cortisol, its own form of cortisone. In 85% of cases, the condition results from a tumor (not usually malignant) in the

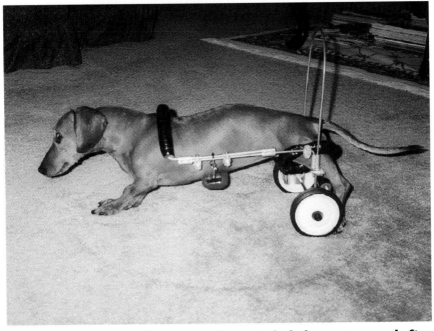

Karen Henry's dog, Sally, uses a K-9 Cart to help her get around after she was stricken with distemper.

pituitary gland of the brain. The remaining 15% arise from tumors (half are malignant) on the adrenal glands, located near the kidneys. The condition is typically seen in middle-aged to old animals, not pups.

There are a lot of different clinical manifestations to Cushing's syndrome but the most common are an increase in thirst, hunger and need for urination. Other clinical signs (symptoms) include hair loss, susceptibility to infection, muscle atrophy and lack of energy. There are several different screening tests for Cushing's syndrome but final confirmation usually relies on a dexametha-sone suppression test or ACTH stimulation test. Treatment for the pituitary disease is most often attempted with mitotane, keto-conazole or L-deprenyl. For adrenal disease, surgery is most commonly utilized or large doses of the medicines mentioned. Cushing's syndrome is more common in the Dachshund but a specific genetic connection has not been determined. Thus, the best means of prevention is to select dogs from families with no history of the disease.

HYPOTHYROIDISM

Hypothyroidism is the most commonly diagnosed endocrine (hormonal) problem in the Dachshund. The disease itself refers to an insufficient amount of thyroid hormones being produced. Although there are several different potential causes, lymphocytic thyroiditis is by far the most common. Iodine deficiency and goiter are extremely rare. In lymphocytic thyroiditis, the body produces antibodies that target aspects of thyroid tissue; the process usually starts between one and three years of age in affected animals but doesn't become clinically evident until later in life.

There is a great deal of misinformation about hypothyroidism. Owners often expect their dog to be obese with the condition and otherwise don't suspect it. The fact is that hypothyroidism is quite variable in its manifestations and obesity is only seen in a small percentage of cases. In most cases, affected animals appear fine until they use up most of their remaining thyroid hormone reserves. The most common manifestations then are lack of energy and recurrent infections. Hair loss is seen in about one-third of cases.

You might suspect that hypothyroidism would be easy to diagnose but it is trickier than

Your Dachshund can look healthy and still have hypothyroidism. Most affected animals look fine until their thyroid hormone reserves are used up.

you think. Since there is a large reserve of thyroid hormones in the body, a test measuring only total blood levels of the hormones (T-4 and T-3) is not a very sensitive indicator of the condition. Thyroid stimulation tests are the best way to measure the functional reserve. Measuring "free" and "total" levels of the hormones or endogenous TSH (thyroid-stimulating hormone) are other approaches. Also, since we know that most cases are due to antibodies produced in the body, screening for these autoantibodies can help identify animals at risk of developing hypothyroidism.

Because Dachshunds have long backs and short legs they are especially prone to intervertebral disk disease.

Because this breed is so prone to developing hypothyroidism, periodic "screening" for the disorder is warranted in many cases. Although none of the screening tests is perfect, a basic panel evaluating total T-4, free T-4 and cholesterol levels is a good start. Ideally, this would first be performed at one year of age and annually thereafter. This "screening" is practical, because none of these tests are very expensive.

Fortunately, although there may be some problems in diagnosing hypothyroidism, treatment is straightforward and relatively inexpensive. Supplementing the affected animal twice daily with thyroid hormone effectively treats the condition. In many breeds, supplementation with thyroid hormones is commonly done to help confirm the diagnosis. Animals with hypothyroidism should not be used in a breeding program and those with circulating autoantibodies but no actual hypothyroid disease should also not be used for breeding.

INTERVERTEBRAL DISK DISEASE

Everyone has heard of a slipped disk, but some may be surprised to learn that this is a common problem in the dog. The Dachshund is the most common breed affected, and by some estimates, this breed may account for up to half of all cases

Long romps in the great outdoors are out of the question for Dachshunds stricken with back problems. This guy doesn't look like he has to worry.

reported. Approximately 85% of herniated disks occur in the lower back, and 15% in the neck region.

The intervertebral disk is like a jelly donut with a tough fibrous outer layer and a jelly-like inner layer. In some instances, the jelly-like inner layer protrudes or "herniates" through the fibrous layer and puts pressure on the spinal cord. This causes intense pain and limited use of the limbs supplied by those obstructed nerves. There can be different reasons for why the disk material herniates and causes such damage. In breeds with stunted legs (chondro-dystrophoid breeds) such as the Dachshund, 75–100% of all disks may be degenerated by one year of age.

The cardinal sign of IVD disease is intense pain. Other signs (symptoms) depend on where the herniation occurred. When a disk ruptures in the neck (cervical disk disease), pain is usually the only problem noted. That's because the spinal cord space is relatively wide there and so there is less chance that the cord itself will become compressed. These dogs will often cry out in pain, and not want their head or neck to be manipulated or moved.

When a disk ruptures in the lower back (thoracolumbar disk disease) the presentation can be much more severe. Often there is paralysis of the hind legs and pressure is applied by the herniated material onto the disk. In a very short period of time, the pain subsides as the spinal cord damage interferes with the ability to recognize pain. These cases are surgical emergencies. Radiographs (x-rays) and some special radiographic studies may be needed to confirm the diagnosis and location of the herniation. Occasionally it will be necessary to inject dye into the spinal canal (myelography) to identify the exact location of the problem.

Intervertebral disk disease can be managed medically or surgically but there are definite guidelines to suggest which is most appropriate. Medical therapy may be adequate when there is mild-to-moderate pain but no evidence of spinal cord damage (e.g., paralysis). Strict cage rest must be enforced and a variety of anti-inflammatory drugs are used to reduce the swelling in the spinal cord. The drug regimen often includes corticosteroids ("cortisone") which works very fast at reducing inflammation in this region. Muscle relaxants may also be prescribed. This form of therapy is most appropriate for dogs with cervical disk disease.

For dogs with thoracolumbar disk disease, paralysis, and loss of deep pain sensation, surgery should be immediate. If the pressure on the spinal cord is not reduced within about 24 hours, permanent nerve damage is likely. Many different surgical techniques are available to "decompress" the spinal canal and remove the herniated disk ma-

terial. At the time of surgery, the surgeon may elect to "fenestrate" other disks in the area that are at risk of future rupture. Since IVD syndrome in chondrodystrophoid breeds is likely to involve more than one disk eventually, this is considered a preventive measure against the need for future surgeries.

Medical therapy can be attempted for thoracolumbar disk disease as long as there is still pain sensation and incomplete paralysis. This suggests that the damage to the spinal cord is more superficial, and less likely to be permanent. Unfortunately, dogs successfully managed with medical therapy have a 40% chance of recurrence. For dogs that have had deep pain loss for over 24 hours, the chances for complete recovery are slim, so

Healthy and sick dogs alike need lots of tender loving care to live satisfying lives.

conservative therapy would be just as effective as surgery in these cases. With perseverance and a dedicated owner, even these animals might regain some function in weeks or months. Many paralyzed Dachshunds can still do well in rolling carts (e.g., K-9 carts) that support their hind end while they continue to use their front legs for locomotion. It is best not to use dogs with a family history of intervertebral disk disease in breeding programs.

MEDIAL PATELLAR LUXATION

The patella is the kneecap and patellar luxation refers to the condition when the kneecap slips out of its usually resting place and lodges on the inside (medial aspect) of the knee. It is a congenital problem of dogs but the degree of patellar displacement may increase with time as the tissues stretch and the bones continue to deform. The condition is seen primarily in small and toy breeds of dogs.

Medial patellar luxation may be graded by veterinarians as to how much laxity there is in the patella. No laxity is preferred and affected individuals may have Grade I (mild) through Grade IV (severe). The diagnosis can be made by manipulating the knee joint to see if the kneecap luxates towards the inner (medial) aspect of the leg. There is usually little or no pain associated with this process. Radiography (x-rays) can be used to document persistent luxation and to evaluate for other abnormalities such as arthritic changes.

Older dogs and those mildly affected may respond to conservative therapy, but surgery is often recommended for young dogs before arthritic changes become evident. There are several successful surgical techniques for this condition. After surgery, dogs should have enforced rest for 6 weeks while healing, and leash activity only. The results are excellent in most cases.

The best form of prevention is to only purchase animals that have no family history of medial patellar luxation. Registries are maintained by the Orthopedic Foundation for Animals (OFA) and the Institute for Genetic Disease Control in Animals (GDC).

NARCOLEPSY

Narcolepsy is a sleep disorder in which animals may spontaneously fall asleep without association to tiredness. Affected pups usually start to have problems between 4 and 20 weeks of age; they often have more attacks as they get excited or try to eat or sleep. The condition can be con-

By getting your puppy from someone whose breeding stock has no
history of medial patellar luxation, you have a better chance of not
having to deal with it yourself.

clusively diagnosed based on food-elicited cataplexy testing should that prove necessary. Various drugs such as yohimbine and imipramine have been used in treatment but many Dachshunds tend to have fewer attacks as they get older.

The condition can be prevented if relatives of affected pups are not used in breeding. This includes normal siblings, parents and their siblings and grandparents and their siblings. Hopefully we'll have a predictive test one day so that potential breeding pairs can be screened, but that is not an option at present.

PROGRESSIVE RETINAL ATROPHY

Progressive retinal atrophy (PRA) refers to several inherited disorders affecting the retina that result in blindness. PRA is thought to be inherited with each breed demonstrating a specific age of onset and pattern of inheritance. The condition has been fairly extensively studied in the miniature longhaired Dachshund but the actual disease gene has not yet been identified. Based on current research, it is predicted to be transmitted as an autosomal recessive trait.

All of the conditions described as progressive retinal atrophy have one thing in common. There is progressive atrophy or degeneration of the retinal tissue. Visual impairment occurs slowly but progressively. Therefore, animals often adapt to their reduced vision until it is compromised to near blindness. Because of this, owners

Your veterinarian will know to check your Dachshund's eyes for progressive retinal atrophy (PRA).

Dr. Henry uses direct visualization of the retina to check Edberg Weinermeister for PRA.

may not notice any visual impairment until the condition has progressed significantly.

In time, dogs will become blind and then the condition is obvious. In the early stages of PRA, night blindness occurs first. Affected dogs may have difficulty navigating themselves at night, or once the lights have been turned off. With progression, some pet owners may notice a characteristic shine from the eye, due to an increased reflectivity of the back of the eye. Because dogs have many other well-developed senses, such as smell and hearing, their lack of sight is usually not immediately evident. The loss of vision is slow but progressive, and blindness eventually results.

The diagnosis of PRA can be made in two ways: direct visualization of the retina, and electroretinography (ERG). The use of indirect ophthalmoscopy requires a great deal of training and expertise and is more commonly performed by ophthalmology specialists than general practitioners. In the miniature longhaired Dachshund, changes are usually evident by 6-12 months of age. An additional highly sensitive test, usually available only from specialists is "electroretinography" or ERG. The procedure is painless, but usually available only from specialty centers. This detects changes by 9 months of age.

There is no cure for PRA and affected dogs eventually go blind. Identification of affected breeding animals is essential to prevent spread of the condition within the breed. Breeding animals should be examined annually by a veterinary ophthalmologist.

SEBACEOUS ADENITIS

Sebaceous adenitis is a recently described inflammatory disease of the hair follicles and the sebaceous glands that supply them. Most animals are in young adulthood when first affected and develop flaking of the skin and then a loss of hair. In general the condition is not itchy or irritating unless the dogs have managed to develop infection in these sites.

Other than these changes, the dogs appear to remain in good health.

For proper diagnosis, biopsies are required and they should be sent to veterinary pathologists with expertise in skin disorders. Therapy of early cases is often attempted with corticosteroids but success is variable. Other treatments being evaluated include vitamin A derivatives (retinoids), antibiotics, cyclosporine and essential fatty acid supplements. Topical treatment is important because the skin becomes very dry and scaly.

This means frequent shampooing with products that help remove surface scale (e.g. tar, salicylic acid, selenium sulfide) and improving the moisture content of the skin with rinses of 50% propylene glycol and various other moisturizers, emollients and humectants. There is no cure and affected animals should definitely not be used for breeding.

VON WILLEBRAND'S DISEASE

Von Willebrand's disease (vWD) is the most common inherited bleeding disorder of dogs. The abnormal gene can be inherited from one or both parents. If both parents pass on the gene, most of the resultant pups fail to thrive and most will die. In most cases, though, the pup inherits a relative lack of clotting ability which is quite variable. For instance, one dog may have 15% of the clotting factor, while another might have 60%. The higher the amount, the less likely it will be that the bleeding will be readily evident since spontaneous bleeding is usually only seen when dogs have less than 30% of the normal level of von Willebrand clotting factor. There are tests available to determine the amount of von Willebrand factor in the blood and they are accurate and reasonably priced. Dachshunds used for breeding should have normal amounts of von Willebrand factor in their blood and so should all pups that are adopted as household pets.

OTHER CONDITIONS COMMONLY SEEN IN THE DACHSHUND

- Atrioventricular Block
- Black-hair Follicular Dysplasia
- Body Fold Dermatitis
- Brachygnathism (long-haired)
- Ceroid Lipofuscinosis
- Cleft Lip/Palate
- Color Dilution Alopecia (Blue)
- Combined Immuno-deficiency
- Corneal Endothelial Dystrophy
- Corneal Epithelial Dystrophy
- Cutaneous Asthenia
- Deafness (dappled)
- Dermoid
- Ear Margin Seborrhea
- Ectopic Cilia
- Entropion
- Estrogen-responsive Dermatosis
- Glaucoma
- Heterochromia iridis
- Juvenile Cellulitis
- Keratoconjunctivitis Sicca
- Leukocytoclastic Vasculitis
- Mandibular Distoclusion (over-bite)
- Mucopolysaccharidosis
- Multiple Ocular Defects (Merle)
- Nodular Panniculitis
- Optic Nerve Hypoplasia
- Pannus
- Pattern Alopecia
- Pemphigus Foliaceus
- Persistent Pupillary Membranes
- Pinnal Alopecia
- Polydontia
- Portosystemic Shunt
- Recurrent Epithelial Erosion
- Seborrhea
- Sensory Neuropathy
- Squamous-cell Carcinoma
- Sterile Pyogranuloma

INFECTIONS & INFESTATIONS

**HOW TO PROTECT YOUR DACHSHUND
FROM PARASITES AND MICROBES**

An important part of keeping your Dachshund healthy is to prevent problems caused by parasites and microbes. Although there are a variety of drugs available that can help limit problems, prevention is always the desired option.

Facing page: A dog's belly and groin area are places where it's easy to spot a flea problem. Little black specks called "flea dirt" are easily visible against pink skin.

FLEAS

Fleas are important and common parasites but not an inevitable part of every pet-owner's reality. If you take the time to understand some of the basics of flea population dynamics, control is both conceivable and practical.

Fleas have four life stages (egg, larva, pupa, adult) and each stage responds to some therapies while being resistant to others. Failing to understand this is the major reason why some people have so much trouble getting the upper hand in the battle to control fleas.

Fleas spend all their time on dogs and only leave if physically removed by brushing, bathing or scratching. However, the eggs that are laid on the animal are not sticky and fall to the ground to contaminate the environment. Our goal must be to remove fleas from the animals in the house, from the house itself and from the immediate outdoor environment. Part of our plan must also involve using different medications to get rid of the different life stages as well as minimizing the use of potentially harmful insecticides that could be poisonous for pets and family members.

A flea comb is a very handy device for recovering fleas from

The cat flea is the most common flea of dogs. It starts feeding soon after it makes contact with the dog.

pets. The best places to comb are the tailhead, groin area, armpits, back and neck region. Fleas collected should be dropped into a container of alcohol which quickly kills them before they can escape. In addition, all pets should be bathed with a cleansing shampoo (or flea shampoo) to remove fleas and eggs. This has no residual effect, however, and fleas can jump back on immediately after the bath if nothing else is done. Rather than using potent insecticidal dips and sprays, consider products containing the safe pyrethrins, imidacloprid or fipronil and the insect growth regulators (such as methoprene and pyripoxyfen) or insect development inhibitors (IDI such as Lufenuron. These products are not only extremely safe, but the combination is effective against eggs, larvae and adults. This only leaves the pupal stage to cause continued problems. Insect growth regulators can also be safely given as once-a-month oral preparations. Flea collars are rarely useful, and electronic flea collars are not to be recommended for any dogs.

To clean up the household, vacuuming is a good first step because it picks up about 50% of the flea eggs and it also stimulates flea pupae to emerge as adults, a stage when they are easier to kill with insecticides. The vacuum bag should then be removed and discarded with each treatment. Household treatment can then be initiated with pyrethrins and a combination of either insect growth regulars or sodium polyborate (a borax derivative). The pyrethrins need to be reapplied every 2–3 weeks but the insect growth regulators last about 2–3 months and many companies guarantee sodium polyborate for a full year. Stronger insecticides such as carbamates and organophosphates can be used and will last 3–4 weeks in the household, but they are potentially toxic and offer no real advantages other than their persistence in the home environment. This is also one of their major disadvantages.

A flea problem extends beyond the dog to his environment, including the house and yard.

When an insecticide is combined with an insect growth regulator, flea control is most likely to be successful. The insecticide kills the adult fleas and the insect growth regulator affects the eggs and larvae. However, insecticides kill less that 20% of flea cocoons (pupae). Because of this, new fleas may hatch in 2–3 weeks despite appropriate application of products. This is known as the "pupal window" and is one of the most common causes for ineffective flea control. This is why a safe insecticide should be applied to the home environment 2–3 weeks after the initial treatment. This catches the newly hatched pupae before they have a chance to lay eggs and continue the flea problem.

If treatment of the outdoor environment is needed, there are several options. Pyripoxyfen, an insect growth regulator, is stable in sunlight and can be used outdoors. Sodium polyborate can be used as well, but it is important that it not be inadvertently eaten by pets. Organophosphates and carbamates are sometimes recommended for outdoor use and it is not necessary to treat the entire property. Flea control should be directed predominantly at garden margins, porches, dog houses, garages, and in other pet lounging areas. Fleas don't do well with direct exposure to sunlight so generalized lawn treatment is not needed. Finally, microscopic worms (nematodes) are available that can be sprayed onto the lawn with a garden sprayer. The nematodes eat immature flea forms and then biodegrade without harming anything else.

TICKS

Ticks are found world wide and can cause a variety of problems including blood loss, tick paralysis, Lyme disease, "tick fever," Rocky Mountain Spotted Fever and babesiosis. All are

A thorough check for ticks before you bring your Dachshund inside should ensure that none get in your house—or stay on your dog long enough to infect him with disease!

Keeping your lawn mowed will keep the tick population at bay. Puppies definitely benefit from well-kept play areas.

important diseases which need to be prevented whenever possible. This is only possible by limiting the exposure of our pets to ticks.

For those species of tick that dwell indoors, the eggs are laid mostly in cracks and on vertical surfaces in kennels and homes. Otherwise most other species are found outside in vegetation, such as grassy meadows, woods, brush, and weeds.

Ticks feed only on blood but they don't actually bite. They attach to an animal by sticking their harpoon-shaped mouthparts into the animal's skin and then they suck blood. Some ticks can increase their size 20–50 times as they feed. Favorite places for them to locate are between the toes and in the ears although they can appear anywhere on the skin surface.

A good approach to prevent ticks is to remove underbrush and leaf litter, and to thin the trees in areas where dogs are allowed. This removes the cover and food sources for small mammals that serve as hosts for ticks. Ticks must have adequate cover that provides high levels of moisture and at the same time provides an opportunity of contact with animals. Keeping the lawn well maintained also makes ticks less likely to drop by and stay.

Because of the potential for ticks to transmit a variety of harmful diseases, dogs should be carefully inspected after walks through wooded areas (where ticks may be found) and careful removal of all ticks can be very important in the prevention of disease. Care should be taken not to squeeze, crush, or puncture the body of the tick since exposure to body fluids of ticks may lead to spread of any disease carried by that tick to the animal or to the person removing the tick. The tick should be disposed of in a container of alcohol or flushed down the toilet. If the site becomes infected, veterinary attention should be sought immediately. Insecticides and repellents should only be applied to pets following appropriate veterinary advice, since indiscriminate use can be dangerous. Recently, a new tick collar has become available which contains amitraz. This collar not only kills ticks, but causes them to retract from the skin within 2–3 days. This greatly reduces the chances of ticks transmitting a variety of diseases. A spray formulation has also recently been developed and marketed. It might seem that there should be vaccines for all the diseases carried by ticks but only a Lyme disease (*Borrelia burgdorferi*) formulation is currently available.

MANGE

Mange refers to any skin condition caused by mites. The contagious mites include ear mites, scabies mites, *Cheyletiella* mites and chiggers. Demodectic mange is associated with proliferation of *Demodex* mites, but they are not considered contagious. Demodicosis is covered in more detail in the chapter on breed-related medical conditions.

The most common causes of mange in dogs are ear mites and these are extremely contagious. The best way to avoid ear mites is to buy pups from sources that don't have a problem with ear mite infestation. Otherwise, pups readily acquire them when kept in crowded environments in which other animals might be carriers. Treatment is effective if whole body (or systemic) therapy is used, but relapses are common when medication in the ear canal is the only approach. This is because the mites tend to crawl out of the ear canal when medications are instilled. They simply feed elsewhere on the body until it is safe for them to return to the ears.

Scabies mites and *Cheyletiella* mites are passed on by other

There's no reason you and your Dachshund can't spend many happy hours together outside without worrying about parasites—preventive measures are the key.

dogs that are carrying the mites. They are "social" diseases that can be prevented by preventing exposure of your dog to others that are infested. Scabies (sarcoptic mange) has the dubious honor of being the most itchy disease to which dogs are susceptible. Chigger mites are present in forested areas and dogs acquire them by roaming in these areas. All can be effectively diagnosed and treated by your veterinarian should your dog happen to become infested.

HEARTWORM

Heartworm disease is caused by the worm *Dirofilaria immitis* and is spread by mosquitoes. The female heartworms produce microfilariae (baby worms) that circulate in the bloodstream, waiting to by picked up by mosquitoes to pass the infection along. Dogs do not get heartworm by socializing with infected dogs; they only get infected by mosquitoes that carry the infective microfilariae. The adult heartworms grow in the heart and major blood vessels and eventually cause heart failure.

Fortunately, heartworm is easily prevented by safe oral medications that can be administered daily or on a once-a-month basis. The once-a-month preparations also help prevent many of the common intestinal parasites, such as hookworms, roundworms and whipworms.

These mini Dachsies are protected against heartworm and parasites thanks to preventatives and vaccines.

Judy Nunes's Doberman, Mugsy, watches over Oscar, her three-month-old Dachshund. Dogs can pass worms to each other, but these healthy dogs won't.

Prior to giving any preventative medication for heartworm, an antigen test (an immunologic test that detects heartworms) should be performed by a veterinarian since it is dangerous to give the medication to dogs that harbor the parasite. Some experts also recommend a microfilarial test, just to be doubly certain. Once the test results show that the dog is free of heartworms, the preventative therapy can be commenced. The length of time the heartworm preventatives must be given depends on the length of the mosquito season. In some parts of the country, dogs are on preventative therapy year round. Heartworm vaccines may soon be available but the preventatives now available are easy to administer, inexpensive and quite safe.

INTESTINAL PARASITES

The most important internal parasites in dogs are roundworms, hookworms, tapeworms and whipworms. Roundworms are the most common. It has been estimated that 13 trillion roundworm eggs are discharged in dog feces every day! Studies have shown that 75% of all pups carry roundworms and start shedding them by 3 weeks of age. People are infected by exposure to dog feces containing infective roundworm eggs, not by handling pups. Hookworms can cause a disorder known as cutaneous larva migrans in people. In dogs, they are most dangerous to puppies since they latch onto the intestines and suck blood. They can cause anemia and even death when they are present in large numbers. The most common tapeworm is *Dipylidium caninum* which is spread by fleas. However, another tapeworm (*Echinococcus multilocularis*) can cause fatal disease in people and can be spread to people from dogs. Whipworms live in the lower aspects of the intestines. Dogs get whipworms by consuming infective larvae. However, it may be another three months before they start shedding them in their stool, greatly complicating diagnosis. In other words, dogs can be infected by whipworms, but fecal evaluations are usually negative until the dog starts passing those eggs three months after being infected.

Other parasites, such as coccidia, *Cryptosporidium*, *Giardia* and flukes can also cause problems in dogs. The best way to prevent all internal parasite problems is to have pups dewormed according to your veterinarian's recommendations, and to have parasite checks done on a regular basis, at least annually.

VIRAL INFECTIONS

Dogs get viral infections such as distemper, hepatitis, parvovirus and rabies by exposure to infected animals. The key to prevention is controlled exposure to other animals and, of course, vaccination. Today's vaccines are extremely effective and properly vaccinated dogs are at minimal risk for contracting these diseases. However, it is still important to limit exposure to other

Dogs who visit strange places where other dogs go, too, have an increased chance of getting worms. They also see more of the world.

This Dachshund contents himself with a Gumabone, a far better pastime than destructive chewing or eating a harmful substance.

animals that might be harboring infection. When selecting a facility for boarding or grooming an animal, make sure they limit their clientele to animals that have documented vaccine histories. This is in everyone's best interest. Similarly, make sure your veterinarian has a quarantine area for infected dogs and that animals aren't admitted for surgery, boarding, grooming or diagnostic testing without up-to-date vaccinations. By controlling exposure and ensuring vaccination, your pet should be safe from these potentially devastating diseases.

It is beyond the scope of this book to settle all the controversies of vaccination but they are worth mentioning. Should vaccines be combined in a single injection? It's convenient and cheaper to do it this way, but might some vaccine ingredients interfere with others? Some say yes, some say no. Are vaccine schedules designed for convenience or effectiveness? Mostly convenience. Some ingredients may only need to be given every two or more years. Research is incomplete. Should the dose of the vaccine vary with weight or should a Dachshund receive the same dose as a Great Dane? Good questions, no definitive answers. Finally, should we be using modified-

If you need to board your Dachshund at any time, make sure the animals he will come in contact with are also vaccinated against common diseases.

live or inactivated vaccine products? There is no short answer for this debate. Ask your veterinarian and do a lot of reading yourself!

CANINE COUGH

Canine infectious tracheobronchitis, also known as canine cough and kennel cough, is a contagious viral/bacterial disease that results in a hacking cough that may persist for many weeks. It is common wherever dogs are kept in close quarters, such as kennels, pet stores, grooming parlors, dog shows, training classes, and even veterinary clinics. The condition doesn't respond well to most medications, but eventually clears spontaneously over a course of many weeks. Pneumonia is a possible but uncommon complication.

Prevention is best achieved by limiting exposure and utilizing vaccination. The fewer opportunities you give your dog to contact others, the less the likelihood of getting infected. Vaccination is not foolproof because many different viruses can be involved.

Parainfluenza virus is included in most vaccines and is one of the more common viruses known to initiate the condition. *Bordetella bronchiseptica* is the

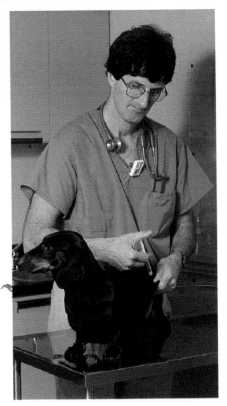

Canine cough, also known as kennel cough, is something all dogs should be vaccinated against, as it is highly contagious.

bacterium most often associated with tracheobronchitis and a vaccine is now available that needs to be repeated twice yearly for dogs at risk. This vaccine is squirted into the nostrils to help stop the infection before it gets deeper into the respiratory tract. Make sure the vaccination is given several days (preferably 2 weeks) before exposure to ensure maximal protection.

FIRST AID
by Judy Iby, RVT

KNOWING YOUR DOG IN GOOD HEALTH

With some experience, you will learn how to give your dog a physical at home, and consequently will learn to recognize many potential problems. If you can detect a problem early, you can seek timely medical help and decrease your dog's risk of developing a more serious problem.

Facing page: When you know your Dachshund well, you'll be able to tell when he's not feeling 100 percent.

Every pet owner should be able to take his pet's temperature, pulse, respirations, and check the capillary refill time (CRT). Knowing what is normal will alert the pet owner to what is abnormal, and this can be life saving for the sick pet.

TEMPERATURE

The dog's normal temperature is 100.5 to 102.5 degrees Fahrenheit. Take the temperature rectally for at least one minute. Be sure to shake the thermometer down first, and you may find it helpful to lubricate the end. It is easy to take the temperature with the dog in a standing position. Be sure to hold on to the thermometer so that it isn't expelled or sucked in. A dog could have an elevated temperature if he is excited or if he is overheated; however, a high temperature could indicate a medical emergency. On the other hand, if the temperature is below 100 degrees, this could also indicate an emergency.

CAPILLARY REFILL TIME AND GUM COLOR

It is important to know how your dog's gums look when he is healthy, so you will be able to recognize a difference if he is not feeling well. There are a few breeds, among them the Chow

Chow and its relatives, that have black gums and a black tongue. This is normal for them. In general, a healthy dog will have bright pink gums. Pale gums are an indication of shock or anemia and are an emergency. Likewise, any yellowish tint is an indication of a sick dog. To check capillary refill time (CRT) press your thumb against the dog's gum. The gum will blanch out (turn white) but should refill (return to the normal pink color) in one to two seconds. CRT is very important. If the refill time is slow and your dog is acting poorly, you should call your veterinarian immediately.

HEART RATE, PULSE, AND RESPIRATIONS

Heart rate depends on the breed of the dog and his health. Normal heart rates range from about 50 beats per minute in the larger breeds to 130 beats per minute in the smaller breeds. You can take the heart rate by pressing your fingertips on the dog's chest. Count for either 10 or 15 seconds, and then multiply by either 6 or 4 to obtain the rate per minute. A normal pulse is the same as the heart rate and is taken at the femoral artery located on the insides of both rear legs. Respirations should be observed and depending on the size and breed of the dog should be 10 to 30 per minute. Obviously, illness or excitement could account for abnormal rates.

PREPARING FOR AN EMERGENCY

It is a good idea to prepare for an emergency by making a list and keeping it by the phone. This list should include:

1. Your veterinarian's name, address, phone number, and office hours.
2. Your veterinarian's policy for after-hour care. Does he take his own emergencies or does he refer them to an emergency clinic?
3. The name, address, phone number and hours of the emergency clinic your veterinarian uses.
4. The number of the National Poison Control Center for Animals in Illinois: 1-800-548-2423. It is open 24 hours a day.

In a true emergency, time is of the essence. Some signs of an emergency may be:

1. Pale gums or an abnormal heart rate.
2. Abnormal temperature, lower than 100 degrees or over 104 degrees.
3. Shock or lethargy.
4. Spinal paralysis.

A dog hit by a car needs to be checked out and probably should have radiographs of the chest and abdomen to rule out pneumothorax or ruptured bladder.

It's important to know how to take your dog's temperature. A healthy dog's temperature ranges between 100.5 to 102.5 degrees Fahrenheit.

EMERGENCY MUZZLE

An injured, frightened dog may not even recognize his owner and may be inclined to bite. If your dog should be injured, you may need to muzzle him to protect yourself before you try to handle him.

It is a good idea to practice muzzling the calm, healthy dog so you understand the technique. Slip a lead over his head for control. You can tie his mouth shut with something like a two-foot-long bandage or piece of cloth. A necktie, stocking, leash or even a piece of rope will also work.

1. Make a large loop by tying a loose knot in the middle of the bandage or cloth.
2. Hold the ends up, one in each hand.
3. Slip the loop over the dog's muzzle and lower jaw, just behind his nose.
4. Quickly tighten the loop so he can't open his mouth.
5. Tie the ends under his lower jaw.
6. Make a knot there and pull the ends back on each side of his face, under the ears, to the back of his head.

If he should start to vomit, you will need to remove the muzzle immediately. Otherwise, he could aspirate vomitus into his lungs.

Clear eyes, a lustrous coat and a gentle expression all indicate good health.

ANTIFREEZE POISONING

Antifreeze in the driveway is a potential killer. Because antifreeze is sweet, dogs will lap it up. The active ingredient in antifreeze is ethylene glycol, which causes irreversible kidney damage. If you witness your pet ingesting antifreeze, you should call your veterinarian immediately. He may recommend that you induce vomiting at once by using hydrogen peroxide, or he may recommend a test to confirm antifreeze ingestion. Treatment is aggressive and must be administered promptly if the dog is to live, but you wouldn't want to subject your dog to unnecessary treatment.

BEE STINGS

A severe reaction to a bee sting (anaphylaxis) can result in difficulty breathing, collapse and even death. A symptom of a bee sting is swelling around the muzzle and face. Bee stings are antihistamine responsive. Over-the-counter antihistamines are available. Ask your veterinarian for recommendations on safe antihistamines to use and doses to administer. You should monitor the dog's gum color and respirations and watch for a decrease in swelling. If your dog is showing signs of anaphylaxis, your veterinarian may need to give him an injection of corticosteroids. It would be wise to call your veterinarian and confirm treatment.

BLEEDING

Bleeding can occur in many forms, such as a ripped dewclaw, a toenail cut too short, a puncture wound, a severe laceration, etc. If a pressure bandage is needed, it must be released every 15–20 minutes. Be careful of elastic bandages since it is easy to apply them too tightly. Any bandage material should be clean. If no regular bandage is available, a small towel or wash cloth can be used to cover the wound and bind it with a necktie, scarf, or something similar. Styptic powder, or even a soft cake of soap, can be used to stop a bleeding toenail. A ripped dewclaw or toenail may need to be cut back by the veterinarian and possibly treated with

This Carrot Bone® from Nylabone® is made with real carrots. Dogs prefer such safe and scrumptious chews to anything dangerous.

antibiotics. Depending on their severity, lacerations and puncture wounds may also need professional treatment. Your first thought should be to clean the wound with peroxide, soap and water, or some other antiseptic cleanser. Don't use alcohol since it deters the healing of the tissue.

BLOAT

Although not generally considered a first aid situation, bloat can occur in a dog rather suddenly. Truly, it is an emergency! Gastric dilatation-volvulus or gastric torsion—the twisting of the stomach to cut off both entry and exit, causing the organ to "bloat"—is a disorder primarily found in the larger, more deep-chested breeds. It is life threatening and requires immediate veterinary assistance.

Bees may flock to food that's outside, increasing the chances of dogs getting stung. Supervise any outdoor feedings.

BURNS

If your dog gets a chemical burn, call your veterinarian immediately. Rinse any other burns with cold water and if the burn is significant, call your veterinarian. It may be necessary to clip the hair around the burn so it will be easier to keep clean. You can cleanse the wound on a daily basis with saline and apply a topical antimicrobial ointment, such as silver sulfadiazine 1 percent cream or gentamicin cream. Burns can be debilitating, especially to an older pet. They can cause pain and shock. It takes about three weeks for the skin to slough after the burn and there is the possibility of permanent hair loss.

CARDIOPULMONARY RESUSCITATION (CPR)

Check to see if your dog has a heart beat, pulse and spontaneous respiration. If his pupils are already dilated and fixed, the prognosis is less favorable. This is an emergency situation that requires two people to administer lifesaving techniques. One person needs to breathe for the dog while the other person tries to establish heart rhythm. Mouth to mouth resuscitation starts with two initial breaths, one to one and a half seconds in duration. After the initial breaths, breathe for the dog once after every five chest compressions. (You do not want to expand the dog's lungs while his chest is being compressed.) You inhale, cover the dog's nose with your mouth, and exhale *gently*. You should see the dog's chest expand. Sometimes, pulling the tongue forward stimulates respiration. You should be ventilating the dog 12-20 times per minute. The person managing the chest compressions should have the dog lying on his right side with one hand on either side of the dog's chest, directed over the heart between the fourth and fifth ribs (usually this is the point of the flexed elbow). The number of compressions administered depends on the size of the patient. Attempt 80-120 compressions per minute. Check for spontaneous respiration and/ or heart beat. If present, monitor the patient and discontinue resuscitation. If you haven't already done so, call your veterinarian at once and make arrangements to take your pet in for professional treatment.

CHOCOLATE TOXICOSIS

Dogs like chocolate, but chocolate kills dogs. Its two basic chemicals, caffeine and theobromine, overstimulate the dog's nervous system. Ten ounces of milk chocolate can kill a 12-pound dog. Symptoms of poisoning include restlessness, vomiting, increased heart rate, seizure, and coma. Death is possible. If your dog has ingested chocolate, you can give syrup of ipecac at a dosage of one-eighth of a teaspoon per pound to induce vomiting. Two tablespoons of hydrogen peroxide is an alternative treatment.

CHOKING

You need to open the dog's mouth to see if any object is visible. Try to hold him upside down to see if the object can be dislodged. While you are working on your dog, call your veterinarian, as time may be critical.

DOG BITES

If your dog is bitten, wash the area and determine the severity of the situation. Some bites may need immediate attention, for instance, if it is bleeding profusely or if a lung is punctured. Other bites may be only superficial scrapes. Most dog bite cases need to be seen by the veterinarian, and some may require antibiotics. It is important that you learn if the offending dog has had a rabies vaccination. This is important for your dog, but also for you, in case you are the victim. Wash the wound and call your doctor for further instructions. You should check on your tetanus vaccination history. Rarely, and I mean rarely, do dogs get tetanus. If the offending dog is a stray, try to confine him for observation. He will need to be confined for ten days. A dog that has bitten a human and is not current on his rabies vaccination cannot receive a rabies vaccination for ten days. Dog bites should be reported to the Board of Health.

DROWNING

Remove any debris from the dog's mouth and swing the dog, holding him upside down. Stimulate respiration by pulling his tongue forward. Administer CPR if necessary, and call your veterinarian. Don't give up working on the dog. Be sure to wrap him in blankets if he is cold or in shock.

ELECTROCUTION

You may want to look into puppy proofing your house by installing GFCIs (Ground Fault Circuit Interrupters) on your electrical outlets. A GFCI just saved my dog's life. He had pulled an extension cord into his crate and was "teething" on it at seven years of age. The GFCI kept him from being electrocuted. Turn off the current before touching the dog. Resuscitate him by administering CPR and pulling his tongue forward to stimulate respiration. Try mouth-to-mouth breathing if the dog is not breathing. Take him to your veterinarian as soon as possible since electrocution can cause internal problems, such as lung damage, which need medical treatment.

EYES

Red eyes indicate inflammation, and any redness to the upper white part of the eye (sclera) may constitute an emergency. Squinting, cloudiness to the cornea, or loss of vision could indicate severe problems, such as glaucoma, anterior uveitis and episcleritis. Glaucoma is an emergency if you want to save the dog's eye. A prolapsed third eyelid is abnormal and is a symptom of an underlying problem. If something should get in your dog's eye, flush it out with cold water or a saline eye wash. Epiphora and allergic conjunctivitis are annoying and frequently persistent problems. Epiphora (excessive tearing) leaves the area below the eye wet and sometimes stained. The wetness may lead to a bacterial infection. There are numerous causes (allergies, infections, foreign matter, abnormally located

Unfortunately, dogs can be allergic or develop allergies to any number of plants.

eyelashes and adjacent facial hair that rubs against the eyeball, defects or diseases of the tear drainage system, birth defects of the eyelids, etc.) and the treatment is based on the cause. Keeping the hair around the eye cut short and sponging the eye daily will give relief. Many cases are responsive to medical treatment. Allergic conjunctivitis may be a seasonal problem if the dog has inhalant allergies (e.g., ragweed), or it may be a year 'round problem. The conjunctiva becomes red and swollen and is prone to a bacterial infection associated with mucus accumulation or pus in the eye. Again keeping the hair around the eyes short will give relief. Mild corticosteroid drops or ointment will also give relief. The underlying problem should be investigated.

FISH HOOKS

An imbedded fish hook will probably need to be removed by the veterinarian. More than likely, sedation will be required along with antibiotics. Don't try to remove it yourself. The shank of the hook will need to be cut off in order to push the other end through.

FOREIGN OBJECTS

I can't tell you how many chicken bones my first dog in-gested. Fortunately she had a "cast iron stomach" and never suffered the consequences. However, she was always going to the veterinarian for treatment. Not all dogs are so lucky. It is unbelievable what some dogs will take a liking to. I have assisted in surgeries in which all kinds of foreign objects were removed from the stomach and/or intestinal tract. Those objects included socks, pantyhose, stockings, clothing, diapers, sanitary products, plastic, toys, and, last but not least, rawhides. Surgery is costly and not always successful, especially if it is performed too late. If you see or suspect your dog has ingested a foreign object, contact your veterinarian immediately. He may tell you to induce vomiting or he may have you bring your dog to the clinic immediately. Don't induce vomiting without the veterinarian's permission, since the object may cause more damage on the way back up than it would if you allow it to pass through.

HEATSTROKE

Heatstroke is an emergency! The classic signs are rapid, shallow breathing; rapid heartbeat; a temperature above 104 degrees; and subsequent collapse. The dog needs to be cooled as quickly as possible and treated immediately by the veterinarian. If possible, spray him down with cool water and pack ice around his head, neck, and groin. Monitor his temperature and stop the cooling process as soon as his temperature reaches 103 degrees. Nevertheless, you will need to keep monitoring his temperature to be sure it doesn't elevate again. If the temperature continues to drop to below 100 degrees, it could be life threatening. Get professional help immediately. Prevention is more successful than treatment. Those at the greatest risk are brachycephalic (short nosed) breeds, obese dogs, and those that suffer from cardiovascular disease. Dogs are not able to cool off by sweating as people can. Their only way is through panting and radiation of heat from the skin surface. When stressed and exposed to high environmental temperature, high humidity, and poor ventilation, a dog can suffer heatstroke very quickly. Many people do not realize how quickly a car can overheat. Never leave a dog unattended in a car. It is even against the law in some states. Also, a brachycephalic, obese, or infirm dog should never be left unattended outside during inclement weather and should

have his activities curtailed. Any dog left outside, by law, must be assured adequate shelter (including shade) and fresh water.

POISONS

Try to locate the source of the poison (the container which lists the ingredients) and call your veterinarian immediately. Be prepared to give the age and weight of your dog, the quantity of poison consumed and the probable time of ingestion. Your veterinarian will want you to read off the ingredients. If you can't reach him, you can call a local poison center or the National Poison Control Center for Animals in Illinois, which is open 24 hours a day. Their phone number is 1-800-548-2423. There is a charge for their service, so you may need to have a credit card number available.

Symptoms of poisoning include muscle trembling and weakness, increased salivation, vomiting and loss of bowel control. There are numerous household toxins (over 500,000). A dog can be poisoned by toxins in the garbage. Other poisons include pesticides, pain relievers, prescription drugs, plants, chocolate, and cleansers. Since I own small dogs I don't have to worry about my dogs jumping up to the kitchen counters, but when I owned a large breed she would clean the counter, eating all the prescription medications.

Your pet can be poisoned by means other than directly ingesting the toxin. Ingesting a rodent that has ingested a rodenticide is one example. It is possible for a dog to have a reaction to the pesticides used by exterminators. If this is suspected you should contact the exterminator about the potential dangers of the pesticides used and their side effects.

Don't give human drugs to your dog unless your veterinarian has given his approval. Some human medications can be deadly to dogs.

This list was published in the American Kennel Club *Gazette*, February, 1995. As the list states these are common poisonous plants, but this list may not be complete. If your dog ingests a poisonous plant, try to identify it and call your veterinarian. Some plants cause more harm than others.

PORCUPINE QUILLS

Removal of quills is best left up to your veterinarian since it can be quite painful. Your unhappy dog would probably appreciate being sedated for the removal of the quills.

With a Nylabone® to keep him happy, your dog shouldn't be tempted by twigs or stems of plants that might prove poisonous.

POISONOUS PLANTS

Amaryllis (bulb)	Jasmine (berries)
Andromeda	Jerusalem Cherry
Apple Seeds (cyanide)	Jimson Weed
Arrowgrass	Laburnum
Avocado	Larkspur
Azalea	Laurel
Bittersweet	Locoweed
Boxwood	Marigold
Buttercup	Marijuana
Caladium	Mistletoe (berries)
Castor Bean	Monkshood
Cherry Pits	Mushrooms
Chokecherry	Narcissus (bulb)
Climbing Lily	Nightshade
Crown of Thorns	Oleander
Daffodil (bulb)	Peach
Daphne	Philodendron
Delphinium	Poison Ivy
Dieffenbachia	Privet
Dumb Cane	Rhododendron
Elderberry	Rhubarb
Elephant Ear	Snow on
English Ivy	the Mountain
Foxglove	Stinging Nettle
Hemlock	Toadstool
Holly	Tobacco
Hyacinth (bulb)	Tulip (bulb)
Hydrangea	Walnut
Iris (bulb)	Wisteria
Japanese Yew	Yew

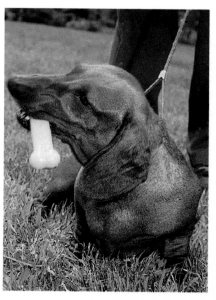

Seizures can last a few minutes or a few seconds. Signs like falling or losing consciousness are serious; this pup is just snoozing.

SEIZURE (CONVULSION OR FIT)

Many breeds, including mixed breeds, are predisposed to seizures, although a seizure may be secondary to an underlying medical condition. Usually a seizure is not considered an emergency unless it lasts longer than ten minutes. Nevertheless, you should notify your veterinarian. Dogs do not swallow their tongues. Do not handle the dog's mouth since your dog probably cannot control his actions and may inadvertently bite you. The seizure can be mild; for instance, a dog can have a seizure standing up. More frequently the dog will lose consciousness and may urinate and/or defecate. The best thing you can do for your dog is to put him in a safe place or to block off the stairs or areas where he can fall.

SEVERE TRAUMA

See that the dog's head and neck are extended so if the dog is unconscious or in shock, he is able to breathe. If there is any vomitus, you should try to get the head extended down with the body elevated to prevent vomitus from being aspirated. Alert your veterinarian that you are on your way.

SHOCK

Shock is a life threatening condition and requires immediate veterinary care. It can occur after an injury or even after severe fright. Other causes of shock are hemorrhage, fluid loss, sepsis, toxins, adrenal insufficiency, cardiac failure, and anaphylaxis. The symptoms are a rapid weak pulse, shallow breathing, dilated pupils, subnormal temperature, and muscle weakness. The capillary

Diligent Dachshunds may get sprayed by skunks while trying to defend their properties.

refill time (CRT) is slow, taking longer than two seconds for normal gum color to return. Keep the dog warm while transporting him to the veterinary clinic. Time is critical for survival.

SKUNKS

Skunk spraying is not necessarily an emergency, although it would be in my house. If the dog's eyes are sprayed, you need to rinse them well with water. One remedy for deskunking the dog is to wash him in tomato juice and follow with a soap and water bath. The newest remedy is bathing the dog in a mixture of one quart of three percent hydrogen peroxide, one-quarter cup baking soda, and one teaspoon liquid soap. Rinse well. There are also commercial products available.

SNAKE BITES

It is always a good idea to know what poisonous snakes re-

side in your area. Rattlesnakes, water moccasins, copperheads, and coral snakes are residents of some areas of the United States. Pack ice around the area that is bitten and call your veterinarian immediately to alert him that you are on your way.

Try to identify the snake or at least be able to describe it (for the use of antivenin). It is possible that he may send you to another clinic that has the proper antivenin.

VACCINATION REACTION

Once in a while, a dog may suffer an anaphylactic reaction to a vaccine. Symptoms include swelling around the muzzle, extending to the eyes. Your veterinarian may ask you to return to his office to determine the severity of the reaction. It is possible that your dog may need to stay at the hospital for a few hours during future vaccinations.

RECOMMENDED READING

DR. ACKERMAN'S DOG BOOKS FROM T.F.H.

OWNER'S GUIDE TO DOG HEALTH
TS-214, 432 pages
Over 300 color photographs
Winner of the 1995 Dog Writers

Association of America's Best Health Book, this comprehensive title gives accurate, up-to-date information on all the major disorders and conditions found in dogs. Completely illustrated to help owners visualize signs of illness, different states of infection, procedures and treatment, it covers nutrition, skin disorders, disorders of the major body systems (reproductive, digestive, respiratory), eye problems, vaccines and vaccinations, dental health and more.

SKIN & COAT CARE FOR YOUR DOG
TS-249 224 pages
Over 200 color photographs
Dr. Ackerman, a specialist in the

field of dermatology and a Diplomate of the American College of Veterinary Dermatology, joins 14 of the world's most respected dermatologists and other

experts to produce an extremely helpful manual on the dog's skin. Coat and skin problems are extremely common in the dog, and owners need to better understand the conditions that affect their dog's coats. The book details everything from the basics of parasites and mange to grooming techniques, medications, hair loss and more.

DOG BEHAVIOR AND TRAINING
Veterinary Advice for Owners
TS-252, 292 pages
Over 200 color photographs
Joined by

co-editors Gary Landsberg, DVM and Wayne Hunthausen, DVM, Dr. Ackerman and about 20 experts in behavioral studies and training set forth a practical guide to the common problems owners experience with their dogs. Since behavioral disorders are the number-one reason for owners to abandon a dog, it is essential for owners to understand how the dog thinks and how to correct him if he misbehaves. The book covers socialization, selection, rewards and punishment, puppy-problem prevention, excitable and disobedient behaviors, sexual behaviors, aggression, children, stress and more.

RECOMMENDED READING

THE DACHSHUND
by Anna Katherine Nicholas & Marcia A. Foy
PS-822, 320 pages
Over 190 full-color photographs
A comprehensive book about one of the world's most popular breeds of dog. Read about the Dachsund's origins, how to raise and care for a Dachshund, the basics of breeding, training, showing and much more. Whether you own a standard or a miniature Dachshund, smooth, longhaired or wirehaired, you'll learn more about your dog reading this book.

THE ATLAS OF DOG BREEDS OF THE WORLD
by Bonnie Wilcox, DVM,
and Chris Walkowicz
H-1091, 896 pages
Over 1,100 full color photographs
If you love dogs you'll love this book. It's the most comprehensive guide to all types of dogs around the world—409 different breeds recieve full-color treatment and individual study. Traces the history and high lights the characteristics, appearance and function of evey recognized dog breed in the world.

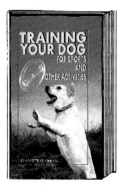

TRAINING YOUR DOG FOR SPORTS
AND OTHER ACTIVITIES
by Charlotte Schwartz
TS-258, 160 pages
Over 200 full-color photographs
In this colorful and vividly illustrated book, author Charlotte Schwartz, a professional dog trainer for 40 years, demonstrates how your pet dog can assume a useful and meaningful role in everyday life. No matter what lifestyle you lead or what kind of dog you share your life with, there's a suitable and eye-opening activity in this book for you and your dog.